A Woman
God Uses

God Bless you!
Much Love

Pam Jenkins

Acts 20: 24

A Woman God Uses

Discovering the road to God's glory

PAM JENKINS

TATE PUBLISHING
AND ENTERPRISES, LLC

Published by Tate Publishing & Enterprises, LLC
127 E. Trade Center Terrace | Mustang, Oklahoma 73064 USA
1.888.361.9473 | www.tatepublishing.com

Tate Publishing is committed to excellence in the publishing industry. The company reflects the philosophy established by the founders, based on Psalm 68:11,
"The Lord gave the word and great was the company of those who published it."

Book design copyright © 2013 by Tate Publishing, LLC. All rights reserved.
Cover design by Rtor Maghuyop
Interior design by Mary Jean Archival

Published in the United States of America

ISBN: 978-1-62510-927-9
1. Religion / Christian Life / Devotional
2. Religion / Christian Life / Women's Issues
13.03.11

Contents

Preface

So that you would walk in a manner worthy of
the God who calls you into His own kingdom
and glory.

—1 Thessalonians 2:12

What if every woman everywhere answered the
call of Calvary, embraced the cross, took up the
cross, carried the cross, stood for the cross, passionately
lived because of the cross, and unashamedly shared the
cross? What if every woman everywhere lived with holy
purpose, walked in tender mercies, served zealously,
worshipped with abandon, praised with passion, prayed
relentlessly, and called upon the name of Jesus full of
faith with great expectancy? What if every woman
everywhere surrendered her all, gave her all, poured
out her all, offered up her all, loved with her all and
lived for God without apology? What if every woman
everywhere lived on the road to his glory? What if that
woman was you?

And the world was never the same.

A Woman God Uses draws from the well of Scripture
to carve out the road that leads to God's glory. Through
the course of this book, each chapter lays out an attribute
found within the life and character of the woman who
journey's this course. These truths will help navigate the
Christian woman who longs to be used by God and
many reasons feels she is not being used, can't be used,

or simply doesn't know where to begin. This book is for any woman of any age, any situation, and any level of spiritual maturity. It's uncompromising in its delivery of truth and compassionately zealous in the pursuit of God's glory. For any woman yearning, thirsty for more of God, or wanting more of the realness of Jesus in her life and more of God's glory radiating through her being, this book is for her. These pages are a product of him, his beauty, his irresistible joy, and his all satisfying calling which is unchanging. His love is unfailing. His tender mercies are discovered upon the narrow road, the road less traveled. For the courageous soul who steps up without apology to surrender herself to his will, and is absolutely abandoned to all that he is, the world will see and will glorify the Father in heaven.

At the Lord's tender bidding have my hands penned the words whispered to my heart by his undeniable voice. He is the perfect one, the sole authority and one deserving of every ounce of glory this author of grace can give back to him. I am his eternal captive; he is my eternal pursuit.

I yearn to be found in him and in him alone. And on that day when every eye shall see, every tongue confess, and every heart understand, may my life resound with glory and praise to the matchless name of Jesus.

This, beloved daughter of God, is why I have written this book.

The Call of the Deep

Deep calls to deep at the sound of Your waterfalls; All Your breakers and Your waves have rolled over me.

—Psalm 42:7

The Psalms are a fortress of strength for every wave of emotion, a shelter for the soul in trouble and a harbor of safety for the fearful. Even though it's not absolutely clear who wrote the forty-second Psalm, it does reveal, with absolute clarity, a heart whose sole desire is for more of God, an undeniable thirsting for the Holy One.

Listen to the yearning heart of the writer, penning words of desperation beginning in the very first verse, "As the deer pants for the water brooks, so my soul pants for You O God." Panting for nothing more than God and yet still for more and more of him. One of the greatest mysteries of the soul is finding God to be all you need yet still finding you need more and more of him.

There is a need so deep, so vast for God, that it will not and can never be filled utterly this side of heaven. The psalmist's soul was experiencing this longing, this deep inexplicable yearning of the deep, a resolve to live and die for God and God alone in want for nothing but more of him. He longed not for merely the Word of God itself, but for the God of the Word—a deepness of soul calling out for the deepness of God, deep calling to deep. Resonate these words upon your heart once more, "Deep calling to deep."

Have you touched the realm of deepness that cries out with such despair for God? You cannot know this deepness until everything you have tried to fill this place with has been stripped away. We must become utterly emptied of all other longings, every other affection before we can experience this deepness of soul. Until we are emptied, completely destitute within ourselves, God will never be our plight, our yearning, our everything. Until every other soul's desire is eradicated, he will never be our sole desire.

What does your heart cry after, run after, yearn for even more than life itself? When you steal away into your secret place of retreat from the hostilities of life, whose arms do you fall into? What is the deepest vein of desire that your soul longs to achieve, to submit, to accomplish? Maybe you've known success in the world's eyes only to find emptiness and longing for something more, but what?

If we could strip away layer by layer the coverings of your heart, what would we see? What words would we hear resounding forth from the deepest recesses? Hear the words of the psalmist once more, "Lord, I cry out to You. I say, 'You are my protection. You are all I want in this life'" (Psalm 142:5, NCV). Is he all you want in this life?

Do you know, really know, what would bring you absolute unbroken happiness? Many have mapped out their course to what they have deemed as their destiny to happiness only to end up dissatisfied, confused, and often times disheartened. What masses have fallen prey to empty dreams, only to find the sun rising, shedding forth a spot light upon the harsh reality of disappointment? How many years of wandering aimlessly in search of life, true life, have you lost in vain? We are all searching for God and for more of God.

In his sweetness, and only as he can do, God orchestrated an appointment with an unbeliever. It was the undeniable hand of Providence that secluded this gift of time together. The conversation was with a young man who had carefully plotted his climb up the corporate ladder to seize the grand prize of more money. He was bright, with great potential, and seemed to know exactly what he wanted from life.

I was amazed to find, even at such a young age, he had all the answers to his life. He had it all planned out, right down to the homemade banner for his life that read, "This way to happiness." He was definitely a man with a big dream on an undeniable mission to be happy with money.

But listening very carefully, I was surprised when he said to me, "But I wonder if and when I reach this goal, if I'll be satisfied. I mean how much money is enough?" A glimmer of doubt began to seep through his own words. This young man had the typical mindset of this generation, self-sufficiency. As long as I'm happy—that's all that matters.

We live in a very goal-oriented, success-driven, happiness-seeking world. And this young man was no different. But in the midst of his pursuits, he was having doubts, second thoughts. It was his deep calling out, no matter how softly, trying to reach the surface, trying to be heard above the noise of the world.

I asked him to give me a definition of what he thought happiness meant. After pondering for a few seconds, he said confidently and matter-of-factly, "Happiness is getting what you want, when you want it." I prodded a teensy bit further by asking him, "But what if someone doesn't know what they want?" You see, he had no idea what he truly wanted.

He looked even more puzzled, trying so hard to salvage his ideology from the frailty of his plans. It was a "light bulb" moment for him, an epiphany. I believe God was calling out to his soul to awaken his need for him. The psalmist knew not only what he needed; he knew what he wanted.

> For a day in Your courts is better than a thousand outside. I would rather stand at the threshold of the house of my God than dwell in the tents of wickedness.
>
> —Psalm 84:10

This is our happiness dilemma, precious one. We are in search of happiness when we don't even know what it is that will make us truly happy. Simply put, we don't know what we want. There is an ever-present underlying fear that if we do find happiness, we won't be able to hang onto it. Is true joy a vacillating reality that God dangles before us in cruelty? Is there hope for our future no matter the amount of loss our hearts have known?

There's good news for all of us. We may not know what we really want, but our Maker does. How does he know this? Because he's the one who designed us, structured our being, and most of all *he designed* the deepest yearning of our souls. He made us to want him. It's our "want factor" that nothing and no one else can fill or even come close to satisfying. Fame, fortune, health, beauty, earthly relationships, positions, success, titles, or awards will never satisfy the need for him.

Etched within every human heart is a lodging place reserved for him, Creator God. This cavern of space is designed to house the throne room of majesty himself, who alone is worthy to govern our life. "As a dry land needs rain, I thirst for You" (Psalm 143:6). Your soul was brought into this world with a thirst for the living God.

Our inner being yearns, craves, and thirsts for intimacy with the one who created us. To know him, to feel him, and experience the nearness of him is the deepest need of mankind. And we will never know the fullness of life, true joy, and enduring happiness until we recognize this need and surrender to it.

Listen to the passion of the heart of the psalmist once more with me, only with a deeper resolve to hear. "As the deer pants for the water brooks, so my soul pants for You. My soul thirsts for God, for the Living God" (Psalm 42:1-2a). The Hebrew word for pants, *arag*, means to cry after, to long for, and it carries the picture of that which is untamed. The writer is very intentional in his word choice as he reveals his untamed desperation in this Psalm. He's painting, without shame, a picture for the world to see, precious daughter, for your eyes and mine.

But what the beautiful artistry is displaying is a life so desperate to get to God that if it doesn't, it will surely die. It's an untamed, wild crazy love for God that is so reckless, so scandalous that it cares not what others will think or say. It's the yearning of God's embrace, the need for the blanket of his presence to cradle them, hold them, and carry them all the days of their life. They would rather die than to be separated from him. It's a need to abandon oneself into the unfailing arms of God knowing he will not refuse them.

This desperate abandonment is painted for us in the life of Peter in John 21. It is the third time Jesus appeared to his disciples after his resurrection from the dead. They were camped near the Sea of Galilee. Peter announced that he's going fishing and wanted the others to go with him. They were out all night long but caught nothing. As the sun was rising upon those sacred waters, a voice was heard calling from the shore line, "Children, you don't have any fish do you?" (John 21:5). They replied back, "No." The voice instructed them to cast their nets on the right-hand side of the boat, and they would find a catch. In so doing, they found their nets full of fish, so much that they could scarcely haul it to shore.

John, the disciple whom Jesus loved, cried out to Peter, "It's the Lord!" Having no self-control (untamed), which I absolutely love about Peter, he put on his outer garment and hurled himself into the sea! Why? Because he couldn't wait to get to Jesus. He had been out all night with the others and was not able to catch anything, but as soon as Jesus came onto the scene, the fish were found in abundance. There was no longer any need for fishing.

When we come to Jesus, when we draw nigh to him, the wants of our lives roll upon the shores of his provision. Peter knew Jesus was all he needed, and to Peter, Jesus was all he wanted.

The beauty is found in what happens next once they reach the shore. Read with me the following verses captured from John 21: 9, "So when they got out upon the land, they saw a charcoal fire already laid, and fish placed on it, and bread." Jesus had what they were in search of! There was never a need to row out into the waters of the world. Jesus was the only waters they needed to delve into. It's a snippet in history that is profoundly relevant for every generation—yours and mine. When we are in want, what waters do we turn to?

They had gone out into the waters of the world, when all along Jesus had what they were working so hard to get. It was only when they came up empty handed that they heard his voice piercing through the emptiness of their boats. Even when we run out into the darkness of night to satisfy our hungry soul, we will always find ourselves wanting in the daytime. While we grope our way through the night, toiling for what we will never find beneath the earthly waters, Jesus is setting his feast upon the shorelines of glory.

I can hear him even now as the weary followers are struggling to make their way back home, calling out, "Children, come to me, I already have what you need." Is it any wonder that Peter threw himself into those sun kissed waters that morning? Jesus knew their emptiness didn't he? While they were out searching, he was preparing their provision. He allows us to lose all to come up empty in our pursuits so we will dive into the waters that will lead us to him, a diving of heart having no other resource, no other way, no other one but him.

Once these hungry souls fed from the Lord's table, they were satisfied. They were filled, and no longer in need of anything. But Jesus didn't stop there. He looked into the very soul of Peter and asked him a question so powerful, so blatant, and so desperate for an answer that Jesus had to ask it three times, "Do you love me more than these?" (John 15:21b). What was Jesus asking Peter? I believe he was asking him for the same confession that we see the psalmist making in Psalm 42:1-2a, "Do you pant for me as the deer pants for the water brooks Peter?" Do you love me more than your trade, more than success, more than ministry, more than your own desires, more than others, more than life itself? Are you desperate for me Peter, truly life altering, self sacrificing, willing to die for, desperate for me?

This was a question only Peter could answer. Jesus knew what lay ahead of Peter, for he goes on to enlighten him a little of what awaits him in his future sufferings. Unless Peter was desperate for Jesus, he would never make it in the times of desperation that were coming. No doubt Jesus's words were seared upon the very heart of Peter that day; words he would need to read aloud over and over again, "Do you love me more than these? Then follow me, run after me, pant for me, pursue me, and abandon yourself to have me at any cost." Peter was given an undying thirst that day, a thirst for more of Jesus, a thirst that the world would never satisfy.

Peter wasn't the only thirsty soul Jesus would confront. In John 4, we see a Samaritan woman who had come to the well to draw water. Day after day, she made her way down the hill carrying her empty water pot to the city's well. Her life was an absolute mess in the eyes of the world. She had been married five times and now living with a man. She was thirsting, longing for something, but she didn't know what. She had tried to find it in men, in worldly relationships.

But this day there was a man waiting for her by the well of water known as Jacob's well. This man wasn't like the others she was used to. He seemed to look right into her soul exposing every secret, every desire, every hurt, and every broken place she had buried so deeply within. Jesus piercing into the core of her conscience speaks these life changing words to her, "Everyone who drinks of this water shall thirst again. But whoever drinks of the water that I shall give him shall never thirst…" (John 4:13–14).

I've pondered many times over the life of this thirsty woman of Samaria. Did she even know how thirsty she was? Did she realize she had a need so great that nothing found in the world would be able to meet it? How many times did she give thought to her past failures? Did she dream of a better day, a different life? Was she longing for something more or had she succumbed to the belief that this was all there was? How many times had she trekked down the path to the well of the world only to come up thirsty? She is the epitome of today's woman, including myself. We are all thirsty; we are all wanting. We are all drinking from some well discovered upon our pathways.

One amazing detail of the Samaritan woman is this: She came carrying her water pot but she left without it. She never drew from the well the day she met Jesus. She is a portrait of the soul who drank deeply of Jesus and never thirsted for things of the world again. It's one thing to come intending to draw; it's another thing to drink.

How many of us head out to draw making a decision to find what we need yet never laying hold of it? We need to see more water pots abandoned by the wells of the earth and more footprints leading away from them to Jesus.

I've held many broken woman in my arms as I prayed with them and listened to their life's journey searching for waters to satisfy the longing of their soul. Some turned to drugs to try and satisfy this longing, some to alcohol, while others turned to sex, and ungodly relationships.

I've witnessed the long road to recovery for women determined to make it out of the pit of destruction they have dug for themselves.

I've watched as others struggled to survive the abuse inflicted upon them by another and then there are those who have continued to drink from the same well that will never satisfy what their soul is so desperate to have, living waters—Jesus. Until we make this confession, we will never discover the divine mysteries that await us with God.

So what's the answer? I believe it's tucked away in a familiar story when Peter and his friends take a fishing trip with a man named Jesus. It was a few years earlier than the previous account mentioned after Jesus rose from the dead. Once again, Peter had been out fishing all night and had rowed back to the shores with empty nets. We find this wonderful event penned in Luke 5:1–11.

> Jesus climbs into the boat of Simon Peter and tells us, "And when He (Jesus) had finished speaking, He said to Simon, "Put out into the deep water and let down your nets for a catch." And Simon answered and said, "Master, we worked hard all night and caught nothing, but at Your bidding I will let down the nets."
>
> —Luke 5: 4–5

Peter had no faith in Jesus's ability to catch fish; he simply obeyed out of respect for the *teacher*. When they rowed out into the deeper waters, they caught such an abundance of fish that Peter had to call for the others to help him. The nets began breaking and the boats were so full of fresh fish that they started sinking in the water. Verse 9 and 11 found in the same passage tells us that "amazement had seized him and all his companions...and they left everything and followed him." What had changed Peter and the others? They were reluctant to obey his voice to follow him in fishing, but now they were unreservedly following Jesus with their lives. Hesitancy had been replaced with abandon. Why? Their waters had changed.

Jesus beckoned Peter to go deeper with him. He had been out in the shallow waters alone and had come up empty, wanting, weary, and discouraged. Peter had tried it on his own, but Jesus was saying, "Now, are you ready to go deeper with me?" Go out into the deeper waters and find in me more than you will ever need. Jesus summons and yearns for all of us to go deeper with him.

What Peter would have missed if he had not yielded to the desire of the Master! It was this experience with Jesus, far away from the shores of life, that changed Peter's life forever. He would never be the same. "O taste and see that the Lord is good" (Psalm 34:8).

The road to his glory begins by answering his call to go deeper with him, to press into him surrendering all within our hands in order to cling wholly to the hem of his garment. He longs to take us away from the crowds, far beyond the shoreline of all distractions until it's just you and him. We may not have the faith, the trust in what he is asking of us but just simple obedience is all he requires, "At your bidding, I will do as you ask." Will that be your hearts reply to the Savior today? Would you venture away from the wide gate where throngs traverse every day that you may enter through the narrow gate where few have dared to tread?

It's a trek not designed for those who are unwilling to let go of all that is dear, familiar, and safe. It demands an awakening of the soul, an awakening that resurrects the dead. It's time for the slumbering soul to open wide the eyes, fixing a gaze upon the horizon until the Son comes into view. "Awake, sleeper, and arise from the dead, and Christ will shine on you"(Ephesians 5:14). Until this awakening happens within us, raising the deadness we have buried beneath our pursuits, we will not know life. We will continue to toil away in the waters of complacency and familiarity never tasting abundant living.

Our souls are aching to live, longing to breathe in all that God is, to pulsate him with every beat of our heart. He calls to each of us, wrapping the cords of his tender mercy round about that we may feel the nearness of his love. His love is all encompassing, unwilling to let go or let up in its pursuit of us. He's asking, precious daughter, he's calling to your heart, prodding you gently to go deeper with him. It's "deep calling to deep."

Oh, the richness and beauty of his glory that awaits us that is revealed, not on the shorelines of the world but out in the stillness of the deep waters, where you find he is all you need; and in the finding, know he is all you want.

Answering this call, this need to have more of God, to have all of Jesus, to commune with him in unbroken dialogue, and to want nothing but more of him. Will you row out with him? Will you bid the world good-bye surrendering everything that is dear to you? You cannot go further with God, you cannot be used more by him, you cannot receive more from him, you cannot experience the depth of him, or know him more until you say, "Yes, Lord, at your bidding will I go deeper with you."

We will never want when we say yes to him. His fullness does not come into our lives in the shallow waters of life. It will not come apart from risks and an all out determination to say yes to him in all things, even when we don't understand, and to pursue him without counting the cost.

The Father is in constant search of the woman in search of him. His eyes are longing to see her, to lay hold of her that she may lay hold of him. He is drawn to her because she draws to him. Listen to the words of the psalmist, "The Lord has looked down from heaven upon the sons of men to see if there are any who understand, who seek after God" (Psalm 14:2). When we look deep into the very heart of this word "seek," we find such beauty in its meaning, "to tread a path to." God looks for footprints, beloved daughter, footprints imprinted upon the dust of his earth leading to him.

Oh, that his eyes would catch a glimpse of that woman who rises while it is still dark, refusing to rest, hastening to the hills of Jehovah God. Oh, that the eyes of God would fall upon a sacred path worn by a life desperate for him. If someone traced the footprints of your life, would they lead them to God? Our lives are designed by God to not only come to him but to leave a trail for others to follow. He is our destination. May we urge the world to take up courage and follow nigh.

Where is that starving soul languishing for God Almighty? Is there a woman so stricken by love for God that will not tolerate the notion of remaining in the courts outside of his throne room, knowing he is just beyond the veil? With all that is within us, we must reach, we must press on to lay hold of him who first laid hold of us (Philippians 3:12). Heaven is longing for the thirsty woman, the woman refusing to settle, striving to reach forward, leaning unto God, aching for his closeness, a woman absolutely lost in his presence. The deepness of God is her one desire, and she will not let up, quit, surrender, fall, turn away, rest, or stop until she has plummeted the holy depths of all that he is.

Until every other desire is released from our grip, he will not become the search of our life. We must acknowledge the greatest need we have—the nearness of God. He is the only one who can satisfy the longing of our heart, the greatest need of our soul. We will never embark upon the supply of God until we first confess our need for God.

If you have a need, a dissatisfaction of the things of the world, it should come as no surprise. You, I, we were made with the deep need for God. Don't mistake this longing for something the world might afford or even that which you could earn with the talent, time, position or money.

Let us dare not to think, even for a moment, that another soul, who has the same deep need for God as you, could possibly be the remedy for the deepest longing within you. Earthly relationships, no matter how precious, can never fulfill the longing your soul has for God. It will not only lead to certain disappointment, but it will heap an insurmountable amount of pressure upon another who is in search of the very same thing you are. If they were the answer, they would certainly not be in desperation to draw nigh to God as you are. One who is in need themselves will never and can never meet the need created within you by God who is never in need.

He's calling from the deepness of himself to the deepness of need found within you. He formed this rarity of space reserving it for himself. It is sealed up unto the day when your cry for him, ascending as a sweet aroma before his face. He beckons you even now to open wide the gate of your heart and cry to him, "More of you, oh God, more of you". He is waiting, longing to pour into the neediness of your being the all-sufficient and all-satisfying power of his presence. But how will you respond? To whom will you give your affections, and where will your footprints lead?

How many of our affections have been laid to waste because they find their lodging in the dearth of the world? We are created for intimacy, intimacy with our Creator. No matter how we choose to meet this need within us for intimacy, it will never be satisfied until we have surrendered all other resources. God must be our source, our way, our hope, our longing, our all. What is God to you? Who is God to you? Is he your way, your future, your rest, your purpose for living? Is he the call from your deepest recess in times of need and in times of peace?

I urge you to write out a confession to the Lord, acknowledging our need for him and our desire to go deeper. It is not a one day journey but a lifelong adventure. Take up the oars, pull up your anchor, and say yes to more of him. Are you thirsty, precious daughter? Are you rowing so desperately out in the waters of life coming up empty time and time again?

Do you hear him calling from the shore line to come home, to jump in without reservation, shame, or fear, and just come? Come as you are, come hungry, come tired, come weary, come wanting, just come. The journey to be the woman God uses begins with this first step. Step out, row out, free yourself from all ties to the shores of the world and let go. Fall into him, and refuse to rest until you get to him.

What would you say to him now? How will you respond to his call—to deep calling to deep? Pen your words to the Living One, oh daughter, and pour out all that is holding you back from giving yourself unconditionally, unreservedly, radical abandonment of self to him.

> Answering the Call of the Deep
> Cry of the Deep…
> Father,
>
> I have run so hard after things that will never satisfy my thirsting soul. I've struggled to find my way, to find happiness and self-fulfillment. I've wandered in waste lands striving for so long when all I needed to do was run to you. Forgive me, oh God, for living as if I did not need you, as if I could meet my deep need for you with other things.
>
> From the depths of my soul, I cry out to the deepness of all that you are. I long for you. My soul is thirsty for the Living God. I cannot make it apart from you. I open wide the gates of my heart and ask you to pour into me the goodness of you. Hear my plea and know that

I long for your nearness to be cradled in the unfailing arms of my heavenly Father.

I love you, Lord, and I know my desperation for you. With arms empty, opened wide, I run to you. Grant me the grace to be found fully abandoned at your feet of mercy.

The Altar of Surrender

The work is great; for the temple is not for man,
but for the Lord God…who then is willing to
consecrate himself this day to the Lord?

—1 Chronicles 29:1,5

David, the son of Jesse, was king of Israel for forty
years. He was Israel's most beloved king and
even greater, he was God's favored one. King David
reigned in Hebron for seven years and in Jerusalem
for thirty-three. The time had come for King David to
pass his royal scepter. The bearer of his crown would be
Solomon, the son born to him by his wife Bathsheba.
It was a joyous time for his majesty to see his bloodline
continue the work of God.

But the work, although a gift and choosing of God,
would be weighty, at times hard yet enduring. The work
was great, and the inexperience of a young king would
be tested. The shoes of the world's greatest warrior
would have to be filled and the holy temple of God
to be built. How would Solomon be able to fulfill the
work God was giving him to do? Where would he find
the strength, the loyalty, and perseverance needed to
accomplish God's plan for his life?

Ready or not, the royal diadem was being passed.
The light of his father's reign was fading quickly, and
the sun was rising upon his. It was Solomon's time to
step forward, extend his hand to the service God had

chosen for him. All of his life, he had been preparing for the day, but was he ready? Questions of "Why me?" and "Can I do this?" surely washed over every facet of his being. This was the position he was created to fill, the ministry written for his life to fulfill.

David, understanding the monumental moment at hand, turned to his people and made a powerful plea petitioning them to make a choice—a life choice. "Who then is willing to consecrate himself to the Lord this day?" The King was looking for a willing soul, a heart that would say yes to his call, yes to building a temple for the Lord. This temple would be shelter for the glory and majesty of God himself. The construction of the temple building was David's lifelong dream, yet he would not be the one to raise it from the earth. This holy rite had been passed over to Solomon by God. It was a bitter sweet moment for David.

From God's anointed came words of inspiration and challenge for the task before them. He knew one powerful truth that set the workman apart from everyone else, "The temple is not for man but for the Lord". But a temple for God could only be built by those who were willing to consecrate themselves, "Who then will consecrate themselves for the Lord's work?"(1 Chronicles 29:5). A consecrated work demands a consecrated workman. Consecration is not forced nor is it a status we can obtain through our works, no matter the goodness or grandeur. Consecration is a choice—a life choice.

This choice is not a token we can reach out and seize with the intent to gain power, notoriety, and fortune or even satisfy the ego of our flesh. At the very core of this choice is death—death to our own agendas, plans, hopes, dreams, opinions, and most of all self. A dying of all that is dear to us, all that makes sense to us, all that brings peace to us and all that we think will satisfy us. There is no "my way," only confessing his way. Is it any wonder the masses are not seeking this way of life? It's the road less traveled, beloved.

When we look deep into the heart of the word "consecrate," we find it to mean "to associate with the sacred." The question King David was asking God's people was, "Who among you is willing to associate with the Holy One, with he who is sacred, worthy, feared, sovereign, with he who alone is God?" This union would demand a separation, a setting oneself apart for the purpose of God. There was a work before them, and if the work was going to be done, it would take a denial of self in order to accomplish the work of God.

Before we can embrace the sacred, we must refuse the common. We cannot associate with the Holy One until we break all ties with the unholy. Listen to God's words uttered to his people in the book of Leviticus, "You shall consecrate yourselves therefore and be holy, for I am the Lord your God" (Leviticus 20:7). God, who is holy, can receive unto himself only that which is holy, only that which has been set wholly apart for him. Once we cross the blessed threshold that takes us from the temporal of our earthly lives into the demesne of heaven, we are declaring our resolve to lay hold of the will of God. This is where the journey begins for the consecrated life.

This step is birthed in the chamber of the heart with an external expression of a life commitment to God. Where there is commitment, there is an altar; and where there is an altar, there is a sacrifice. An altar precedes commitment, and if not, there will soon be an abandonment of the promise made and thievery of God's glory. Every act committed by the consecrated life will be living proof that an altar of surrender is in place. The altar of surrender is erected, not by the hands of the flesh but by hands of surrender that have recognized the worthiness of God. There is but one sacrifice needed upon the altar of surrender, self. It's the sacrifice the Father searches for, longs for, waits for. The altars of surrender lay barren in our land, precious friend, and the glory of God is fading among the ruins.

Self will not approach the altar of surrender joyously and never without a struggle. Self will not yield its rights. It will always seek to survive because of its nature. It's this struggle to preserve life that many yield to never making it to the altar of surrender, missing the consecrated life God longs to see in us. God wants all of us to belong to all of him. He will not take it from us, for he is too much of a gentleman for that. His greatest delight is when his child approaches the altar longing to give everything, unreservedly and wholly to God.

Death of self is the sweetest burial before the throne of the Father. The loam of the burial ground becomes fertile soil now able to receive the provisions, the blessings, and truth that comes from God. He longs to give us life in full measure, but death must take place before life can begin. Most Christians will never experience the life that is used by God because they are unwilling to experience death of self, unwilling to come to the altar of surrender. The tragedy of this—the temple of God will never be built.

The first temple was built by man, but the last will be built by God. See with me, the temple of God is building today as revealed to us in Holy Scripture.

> For we are the temple of the living God; just as God said, "I will dwell in them and walk among them; and I will be their God, and they shall be My people.
>
> "Therefore, come out from their midst and be separate," says the Lord. "And do not touch what is unclean; And I will welcome you. And I will be a father to you, and you shall be sons and daughters to Me," says the Lord Almighty.
>
> —2 Corinthians 6:16–18

Did you hear it, beloved, did you see it? Did your mind perceive the place of the temple today? It's you, his daughter, his bride, his treasure and delight.

In the deepness of God, there is a longing of heart to make your heart his home. His heartbeat pulsates, longing to have your heart, to hear it beating in perfect rhythm with his; to draw you up so near, so intimate that only one heartbeat is heard. God fashioned your heart with his own hands knowing every detail. He knows the closer your heart is to his, the more in *synch* it will be to his own. He designed you this way. This is why we must guard our hearts so diligently, because the heart is pliable to its surroundings. It is designed to conformity.

This living temple is built with one surrender…one separation at a time. With every surrendered sacrifice, a wall is raised and wall by wall God will build a house to display his beauty and glory. What a beautiful woman he will make of you when you become God's dwelling place, the temple to house his presence. May we hear the timely words of King David once again, "Who among you will consecrate himself unto the Lord, for the temple belongs not to man but to the Lord." Solomon would learn from the wisdom of his father that the temple would not be built without an altar.

Gracing the pages of Holy Scripture, you will find the altar of surrender approached by those who answered the call of consecration. Ordinary lives that refused to settle for the ordinary. You won't find these altars among the masses. They are hidden upon the mountainsides of pain and suffering. They are but ruins authenticating the beauty that once took place upon the soil of reckless abandon. The pathways leading to these holy mounds are stained with tears, for they have cost the sojourner everything.

We must put all that we are, all that we have, into the hands of God for him to do with as he pleases. Make no mistake, his gift of life to us is never ours to use as we see fit; it is ours to offer back to God—to give in full measure to use as he desires. We cannot embrace the will of God for our lives until we have utterly let go of ours. The more we surrender, the more God will use us.

James 4:7 calls for this surrender saying, "Submit yourselves to God." The writer saw the beauty and necessity of full surrender, total unwavering submission to God in all things. True life is found nowhere but in the core of his holy will which is always grander than anything we could think or imagine it to be. Jesus said, "He who has lost himself for my sake, will find it" (Matthew 10:39). Until we are lost for Jesus, we will never find the life he longs to give us. Show me a woman who is used by God, and I'll show you a woman who has lost her life to him. Until we choose to lose, we will never win.

Throughout history, we see God crying out, searching for the willing heart, the soul that will follow him, his way and his schedule. He called out Seth from among his brothers Cain and Abel. He called out Shem from the sons of Noah. From Shem, he would beckon Abraham, Isaac from Ishmael, and Jacob from Esau. God was constantly narrowing his search, deepening his calling, narrowing his voice down to Jacob's son Judah, through which King David would come, and in time, our Savior Jesus Christ. Each and everyone set aside, separated, surrendered, and consecrated unto God.

Would God consider you a consecrated woman, a woman totally surrendered to him? Is there an altar of surrender in your life that bears witness of your holy commitment to your heavenly Father? What or who has your heart, your affections, and pursuits? God is constantly narrowing down our life until all that's left is him. There is always one chief principal that God follows in this selective process; he always *includes* the surrendered heart in his work.

God desires for us to be an effectual instrument for the working of God in human history. The mighty men who gathered about David and shared his exile, ultimately became the leaders in his kingdom. It's the same with our King. We must be willing to be exiled with him before we can serve in his kingdom. There are many women who desire to be used by the Lord but are unwilling to be exiled with him. I love this quote from Oswald Chambers concerning Charles Cowman, "The thing that strikes you about Charles Cowman is not his holiness, but his absolute reckless, careless, defiant abandonment to Jesus Christ."

With every consecrated act, we avail our lives, our energies, resources, talents, time, and our all to the power of heaven. This availing is what not only gives increase to the kingdom of God, but our eternal future with crowns that one day will be given as an offering of love to him. The questions remain the same, resounding, life-altering questions that you and I must give an answer to one day not long from now: What did you choose to do with the life God gave you? Will you be found having given it back to him as a fragrant offering of worship?

As self is laid down upon the altar of surrender, something stunning begins to take place. God starts the flame of love upon his costly and most precious offering. His fire begins to burn away all that is earthly, all that competes for his glory, and all that will have no bearing on eternity. The smoke of your offering ascends upward, slowly with sacred wonder unto the hills of Jehovah. There its lodging place is found as it lingers with such sweetness before the face of God. He examines this costly vapor of love. He breathes it in and savors the moment as all heaven declares, "the earthly has united with the Sacred."

But he doesn't stop here, precious daughter. He rises from the throne of power flowing with grace and tender mercy. He stoops down, drawing nigh to the place of sacrifice. And with all that he is, he extends mighty hands of love to scoop up the ashes of your offering found upon the altar of surrender. And, oh beloved daughter, listen to what God will do with the ashes of your offering:

> To grant those who mourn in Zion, giving them a garland instead of ashes, the oil of gladness instead of mourning, the mantle of praise instead of a period of fainting. So they will be called oaks of righteousness, the planting of the Lord, that He may be glorified.
>
> —Isaiah 61:3

He gives beauty for your ashes! What we surrender to God upon the altar of consecration will never end in ashes. Only God can take up the ashes and create beauty unto himself.

Even the potter when working with his masterpiece of clay will remove the ashes from the fire of his kiln, knowing how valuable they are to his earthen vessel. These ashes are the remains of what has been carved away from the vessel of clay. They represent all that was lost, removed from the life of the pottery. With brush in hand, he dips into the ashes that have been kindled in the fire, and with purposeful, skillful strokes of mastery he begins to give beauty to his beloved clay.

The ashes of the clay become the paint of color that will impart beauty to the vessel. It's what will set his vessel apart from every other.

The markings and beauty of the clay are a display of the workmanship of the Master, so when the world beholds its glory, the world will reply, "This is the Lord's doing, and it is marvelous in our eyes." But the clay must yield to his fire, to his wheel, to the pressure of his hand upon it, surrendering with every touch. This is consecration in visible form for us, and it's marvelous. We must refuse to settle for anything less than absolute, complete surrender of all that we are, all that we have, all that we want, and give our very lives to God. Listen to the words of Elisabeth Elliot, "If my life is broken when given to Jesus, it is because pieces will feed a multitude, while a loaf will satisfy only a little lad."

"Consecration" is a word scarcely heard in Christendom anymore. It's uncomfortable, unpopular, and costly. What is it that you have not laid upon the altar of surrender unto God? Maybe it's your very life having never accepted Christ as your Savior and confessing him as Lord. It may be that you are a Christian but have savored parts of your life for yourself, refusing to give them to God. Do you refuse to surrender simply because you don't believe God can or will accept your offering?

Are you afraid to give God your most precious things, those relationships, positions, your job, home, health, career, ministry and life to him because you don't know if you believe he will do what's best with them? Do you fear you've wasted too much time, done too much, have nothing to offer, or that God will reject your precious offering? Listen to these words of the psalmist in light of all that you have read:

> What shall I render unto the Lord for all his benefits toward me? I shall lift up the cup of salvation, and call upon the name of the Lord. I shall pay my vows unto the Lord now in the presence of all his people. Precious in the sight of the Lord is the death of his saints.
>
> —Psalm 116:12–15

These verses give greater meaning to death for us, doesn't it? I believe the psalmist was speaking about a death of self, a surrendered life, not a physical dying because of the content of these verses. He's asking, "What shall I render [sur-render] to the Lord for all his benefits toward me?" He follows with words of great delight for all who decide to surrender to God what he's worthy to receive, which is all "precious in the sight of the Lord is the death [surrender] of his saints." God will consider any offering of your life as dear to him, valued, honored, and treasured. Have no fear in giving yourself, all that you have, all that you are; all that you hope to him, and it will become a treasure, priceless, and beautiful in his hands.

I implore you to approach the altar of surrender and with a heart of complete trust, lay yourself down. He's waiting for you. You can trust him with even your most precious treasures. Won't you lay it all down, my precious sister? Oh, the captive beauty that yearns to be set free through surrender that it may resound in glory and praise to God the Father.

As we close this chapter of our journey, please know that it's only the pages of concentration that close today. Page by page of your life, even those that have already turned and those yet to be turned, are turned over one at a time. Some pages are more painful to turn over than others. It will be a day by day surrender at the altar of God. Consecration is a lifelong journey. Jim Elliott said, "That which is lifelong can only be surrendered in a lifetime." Jim Elliott's life, although laid down very young for the work of the Lord, continues to radiate the beauty of God into the lives of his people. Will you be that consecrated woman? Will you join me upon the path that few will ever venture to trod?

Write out a prayer of consecration to God laying out all that you are giving him today.

My Altar of Surrender Prayer:

_____

_____

_____

_____

_____

_____

_____

_____

_____

_____

I want to close out our chapter together by sharing with you a portion of the consecration hymn.

> Take my will, and make it Thine; it shall be no longer mine.

> Take my heart, it is Thine own; it shall be Thy royal throne.

> Havergal, Frances Ridley. *Evening Melodies.* Philadelphia: Henry Altemus Company, 1900.

A Heart for Holiness

Behold, the Lord's hand is not so short that it cannot save; nor is His ear so dull that it cannot hear. But your iniquities have made a separation between you and your God, and your sins have hidden His face from you so that He does not hear.

—Isaiah 59:1–2

Summers in Georgia are sweltering hot, stiflingly humid and unbearably long! Ask anyone who has spent time in the South, and they will give you a hearty concur, no doubt. It's not the heat so much that gets you, but rather it's the humidity which makes it feel like it's ten times hotter than what it really is. Even though the summers are hot here, they make for some great memories. Kids riding their bikes, running through the sprinklers in the back yard, or headed for the neighborhood pool for a refreshing swim. It calls for ice cold watermelon or homemade churned ice cream with freshly picked peaches. Fans are a necessity and folks take late afternoon walks or visit with neighbors on the front porch swing. Summer time makes for long, lazy days for some and fun-packed days for the youngsters.

It was one of those long hot summer days, and I was about ten years old. Like most kids, I loved the outdoors and as soon as the sun shone its face, I was out the door not to be seen again until I heard my mother's voice calling me in for supper. Hyper was my middle name, and I had no idea what the word "patience" meant. The neighborhood gang was waiting on their fearless freckled leader to come out and give the plan for the day. I grabbed my favorite drinking glass from the cabinet. It was my "happy glass" as I affectionately called it because it was covered in smiley faces. I hurriedly filled it with some good ole sweet southern tea and bounded out the door. I was stopped dead in my tracks with a stern warning from my stepfather, "If you come home without that glass, you are going to get a spanking." Well, of course I was going to bring it home! At least that was my plan at that moment.

I played as hard as any kid could that day and as usual, as the sun began sinking downward, I heard my mother's voice. Her call had a way of echoing through the neighborhood, resounding through every street finding its resting place in my ears. It could find me anywhere, no matter how far away I was from our house. It was like a hound sent out by my little mama to sniff me out and bring me home. I ran home like the wind, mainly to show out in front of my buddies, but also because I was famished from all the hard playing. Unfortunately, super girl forgot one thing—the smiley face glass. I not only forgot to bring it home, but that glass was a long forgotten memory by this point. As I darted through the kitchen to make my way to wash up, I heard a voice call from the garage, "Pamela Joy, did you bring that glass back home?" My heart dropped to my dirty little feet realizing I was in deep trouble.

I knew what was coming—a switch spanking! I was summoned to the garage and after a lengthy interrogation, it was followed by a lecture on responsibility. Then I was sent out to the backyard "to fetch a switch off the bush." I hated switches more than anything and having to go and cut your own somehow made it worse. To a kid, it was like the walk of death! As I made my slow agonizing descent to the lower back yard, I began to ponder a few things: "Was it worth it?," "Would I ever see my favorite smiley face glass again?," and the big one, "How many licks am I going to get this time, and can I pick a little switch and get away with it?" Needless to say, I learned a valuable lesson that day—when I do not obey, I will suffer the consequences. No doubt, I had received some painful corrections before that day, but this is the one that stands out in my memory as a life lesson. Bad decisions can bring pain into your life.

We all have memories of our childhood stored away, some good and some not so good. I knew right from wrong, but growing up I chose to do a lot of wrong. I didn't understand why I made the decisions I did until I became a Christian and began growing in my faith. There is a very small yet destructively powerful word we all know called *sin*. We are born in it and we die with it. It never leaves us, but it will most definitely forsake us; unfortunately, it longs to be our lifelong friend sticking closer than any brother! There are many definitions for sin that I could give at this point, but I've come to understand a very simple meaning. Sin is much more than doing what is wrong; it's the absence of doing what is right—"right" meaning what is pleasing before the eyes of a Holy God. There is a "right" before the eyes of God, our own eyes, the eyes of others and the eyes of the world. Out of all the eyes we live in front of, his eyes are the only ones that matter in eternity.

Learning what is pleasing to him is not always as simple as seeing things in black and white, right or wrong. Listen to the Apostle Paul's words to the church at Ephesus, "For you were formerly darkness, but now you are Light in the Lord; walk as children of Light (for the fruit of the Light consists in all goodness and righteousness and truth), trying to learn what is pleasing to the Lord" (Eph 5:8–10). The longer you journey with God, the clearer this truth will unfold with understanding. The beloved apostle had come to the place in his spiritual life, where he understood that pleasing the Lord was a lifelong journey of commitment day by day, moment by moment. Trying implies work, loyalty, and dedication to a God, who has your heart because you have his. King David prayed, "Teach me thy way, O Lord; I will walk in Thy truth. Unite my heart to fear Thy name" (Psalm 86:11). King David had a hungry heart, a soul thirsting to please God, so he did all he knew to do. He cried out for unity, a oneness of heart. He made a bold and life-changing request by asking Holy God to unite his heart with his own heart, which was unholy—holiness uniting with sinful flesh.

Holiness is what God desires from us because he longs to unite his heart with our own. When he finds a heart offering up a prayer to be united with him, it is as much a delight as ever to him. Isaiah 65:24 makes this declaration, "Even before they call He answers." God's provision precedes our needs. His provision is waiting to be unleashed through our prayers. Anticipating this prayer, this cry to be pleasing to him, to be holy as he is holy, God answered ahead of time by offering Jesus. But God is still waiting today, listening, yearning to receive this call from his child. Would he hear it from you, beloved daughter? Do you desire to be pleasing to him, to be holy as he is holy?

In a sincere exhortation to all those who had accepted Jesus Christ as their Lord and Savior, the Apostle Peter pens these words:

> But the day of the Lord will come like a thief, in which the heavens will pass away with a roar and the elements will be destroyed with intense heat, and the earth and its works will be burned up. Since all these things are to be destroyed in this way, what sort of people ought you to be in holy conduct and godliness.
>
> —2 Peter 3:10–11

Peter was stirring up their faith by way of reminder; the life lived upon the earth will come to a rapid and unexpected end just like a thief who comes in the night. These are sobering words for all Christians knowing that someday it will be too late for repentance, too late for commitment, too late for service and dedication, and too late to please God this side of heaven. Knowing this end, Peter asks a heart probing question, "What sort of people ought you to be in holy conduct and godliness?"

There must be a reverential fear of God before our eyes, or there will be no fear of sin in our lives. We live in an era of history where sin is rampant, and there is no shame in it. It's committed openly and without fear of consequences because there is no fear of God before the eyes of this generation. When we search the Scriptures for a heart that feared God and was committed to personal holiness, we don't have to look long before we find an ordinary man by the name of Job. He was a man who loved and feared God so much that he offered up sacrifices not only for his sins but for the sins of his children continually. Job was a father of seven sons and three daughters, whom he loved very much. But Job had a greater love, a stronger bond with another than even his own family, as dear as they were to him. It was with his God. He guarded his heart with such diligence allowing nothing to take it captive, nothing to entice it away from the one he loved. Proverbs 4:23 warns us to, "Watch over your heart with all diligence, for from it flow the springs of life." We are made privy to this heart in Job 1 that says,

> His sons used to go and hold a feast in the house of each one on his day, and they would send and invite their three sisters to eat and drink with them. When the days of feasting had completed their cycle, Job would send and consecrate them, rising up early in the morning and offering burnt offerings according to the number of them all for Job said, "Perhaps my sons have sinned and cursed God in their hearts." Thus Job did continually.
>
> —Job 1:4–5

The words "thus Job did continually" are an anthem for his love pledge to God, a pledge to keep himself pure, pleasing God in every area of his life including his children's lives. He had a reverential fear and unwavering love for the Lord and nothing would keep him from being absolutely right before him. This is the birthing ground for the vessel God will use to display his glory to all the earth. Capture this spiritual secret, precious daughter, and fetter your heart to its significance.

Uninterrupted dialogue with God was the desire of his heart, and Job knew that sin would break that dialogue. We began our chapter with the prophet's words, "Behold, the Lord's hand is not so short that it cannot save; nor is His ear so dull that it cannot hear. But your iniquities have made a separation between you and your God, and your sins have hidden His face from you so that He does not hear" (Isaiah 59:1–2). God's people had blocked the current of God's favor upon their lives keeping good things from their reach. They had shut themselves off from the blessings God desired so greatly to give to them because of their sins. We are often puzzled when we find our prayers bouncing off our ceilings and slamming back in our face, wondering why God isn't answering. It may be that God isn't answering because he isn't hearing. Sin acts as a partition or sound barrier separating us and our prayers from God. It hides the face of God from us. Sin is more costly than we will ever come to know this side of God's heaven.

Known as the *weeping prophet*, Jeremiah wrote, "Your iniquities have kept good things from you" (Jeremiah

5:25). If our prayers are hindered, then won't also our provision be? Sin is the thief of the good that God desires to pour into our lives. God will not withhold any good thing from those who ask, but the one asking must be first heard. There is an attitude in Christendom that teaches so strongly of the free unconditional grace of God that it removes the seriousness of sin from the picture. As abundant and free as God's grace is, it was never intended to wash away the fear of sin before our eyes. God is not just concerned with our escaping the consequences of sin. The gift of God's forgiveness carries with it moral implications; it does not give us a free pass to live as we want. The world is flooded with religious messages offering forgiveness without transformation, which is not only a dishonor to the cross of Calvary but a travesty against the soul God longs to use.

We must not reduce the gospel's message to a mere way of escape for the regrets of our past. God looks for the heart that has looked with unveiled eye upon the deepness of its own sin, felt the weight it carries, and believed in the cost of it. He searches for the one who makes no excuses but wholly embraces the responsibility of personal sin. Before this can happen, we must look to the holy hill, where the high and lofty one dwells. Just as Isaiah did declaring upon the holy hill, "I am unclean...I am undone" (Isaiah 6:7). The soul that has caught a glimpse of the pure brilliance of the most high God in all his loveliness and untold glory will never look at sin the same. What a rarity this precious soul is in the eyes of God. And how does he react to such a one? He lays hold of us as a vessel fit for the Master's use, just as he did with Isaiah.

God longs to move towards us upon waves of unmerited mercy and unfathomable grace but has, countless times, been turned away at the portal of our life because we refuse to acknowledge the depth and penalty of our sin. God has no choice but to withdraw his gracious presence from us, suspending his marvelous tokens of favor, the power of his strength, and the faithfulness of his help when sin is protected as an object of our worship. We long to see his face through the eye of Scripture, but we find our vision blurred, even blinded to spiritual beauty. Although he is our God, ours by profession, he is much more than a God who saves the lost, forgives the sinner, and eradicates our past. He is holy, sinless, righteous Judge and the Sovereign over the universe and the Creator of all living things. He is deserving of nothing less than for his daughter to acknowledge he is worthy of a clean and holy vessel.

Every sin we allow into our lives withdraws our allegiance from God. It provokes him to hide his face and turn his countenance away in disdain. He will refuse to be heard and to hear. Sin is far more costly to us in the heavens than we ever will know or anticipate upon God's earth. Sin is exceedingly hurtful and profusely costly for all of us. No matter who we are, sin can and will destroy everything we hold dear. It's always looking for a willing ally to work through producing bitter fruit of soul. The writer of Hebrews writes, "Let us also lay aside every encumbrance, and the sin which so easily entangles us and let us run with endurance the race that is set before us" (Hebrews 12:1). The heart of a woman or man is easily tangled up in the sin that has set its sights upon us. It's a pursuing snare of every believer. It is relentless in its hunt for a victim—a victim who will give it lodging. It is the adversary of the Spirit but the friend of the flesh. It exerts strong influence over us, suggesting things to us, commanding our emotions, giving no rest until it takes hostage our affections. It wants all of us, as God does, waging war against the soul.

Sin comes from behind, pushing and driving us forward, never leading, always driving with excessive might. It displays unlimited power, exerting tremendous strength against the weakness of our flesh which is easily overcome. Sin searches for a receptive environment to take up residency. It is a force seeking to have sway with us and one that we will contend with until we are in heaven. But God is looking for that heart that has purposed not to sin against him. Psalm 119:32 says, "I shall run the way of Thy commandments, for Thou will enlarge my heart." The psalmist was going to run the path of obedience declaring his heart for pleasing God. He is very purposeful in his choosing of the path he will run—the road he will tread, and nothing less than God's Way would do for him. Oh, how few have chosen the way to his glory, the pathway to usefulness for the kingdom of God!

A year or so ago, I discovered the story of a little animal called the ermine. I had never heard of an ermine before, so I was intrigued with what I was reading. This little creature is part of the weasel family and makes its habitat in the northern regions of Europe. It's covered with soft, snow-white fur with the exception of a black tip on the end of its tail. It measures only about five to ten inches in body length. These beautiful tiny creatures are prized by hunters, for their fur is used to make women's coats and other things. This fur is also used for the trimming found around the robe of judges because it's symbolic of purity and honor. When looking closely at the habits of the ermine, you come to realize why this symbolism is so prized.

This ermine takes great pride in its fur coat, taking every precaution possible to keep its snowy white fur from being soiled. The ermine is difficult for hunters to catch, so they devised a plan around the ermine's lifestyle of cleanliness. They scout out the home of the ermine, and once it has left its den, they will dirty the entrance way and around the outside of the entrance with filth from the earth. The hunting dogs will pursue the ermine, knowing it will head to its home in order to seek refuge. But a remarkable thing happens when the hunting dogs arrive at the entrance of the ermine's den; they find that the ermine has not entered for safety but rather it is found trembling outside the door of safety. Why would the ermine not run into the safety of its home to escape the jaws of death? Because the ermine would rather die than soil its white coat.

What a striking life picture God has given to us through the life of a seemingly insignificant little weasel. Isn't that just like God to use a weasel to challenge us to a commitment of purity? If we would guard our purity in such a way, deeming it as more precious than life itself, what wonders God would do through us? Sin doesn't pass in and out of lives without leaving its mark upon us. Sin soils our lives, ruins our testimony before others, and brings dishonor to the robes of righteousness we have been given by God. Listen to the words of Peter:

> Conduct yourselves in fear during your stay upon earth; knowing that you were not redeemed with perishable things like silver or gold from your futile way of life inherited from your forefathers, but with precious blood, as of a lamb unblemished and spotless, the blood of Christ
>
> —1 Peter 1:17–19

Purity in the life of a Christian should be guarded and never surrendered even if it costs us our life. This kind of steadfast purpose in our life is essential, vital if we are going to be the woman God can use. Will you be that woman? Are you that woman? What sin has entangled you, precious daughter, that has kept you from God's glory? It begins with confession. 1 John 1:9 declares a wondrous hope for all who acknowledge their sins to God, "For if we confess our sins, He is faithful and just to forgive us our sins and to cleanse us from all unrighteousness." What hope for all our failures, those in the past, present, and yet to come! What security for our future! God cannot secure our future until he reconciles our past.

So what women ought we to be? What pursuits have we embarked upon and taken a full assessment of what or who is pursuing us? We can be so busy with our own pursuits that we fail to notice the one treading so softly yet so intently behind us. Cain, the son of Adam and Eve, brother to Abel, became the hunted in the face of sin. Read with me the words of God spoken to him:

> So Cain became very angry and his countenance fell. Then the Lord said to Cain, "Why are you angry? And why has your countenance fallen? If you do well, will not your countenance be lifted up? And if you do not do well, sin is crouching at the door; and its desire is for you, but you must master it."
>
> —Genesis 4:6–7

The word "desire" as used in verse 7 of this passage means "to tread down, or overtake". God was using pretty strong verbiage with Cain wasn't he? He describes sin as a hunter whose goal is to tread us down and master the captive. God was giving Cain a warning letting him know that sin was after him, and it was just outside his door lying in wait for the perfect opportunity to strike.

We must not welcome the unclean. We must not give it passage into our life. When we do not refuse it, we welcome it, and when we welcome it, we agree with it. Entertaining sin can be just as destructive as remaining in sin. You cannot pursue the path of holiness lingering in the lowlands. Hear the words of God spoken thousands of years ago yet breathed into our generation—into our very being:

> Therefore, come out from their midst and be
> separate, says the Lord. and do not touch what
> is unclean; and I will welcome you, and I will
> be a father to you, and you shall be sons and
> daughters to Me, says the Lord Almighty.
>
> —2 Corinthians 6:17–18

My heart rejoices every time I read these words, "And you shall be sons and daughters to Me." God is promising to be a father to me! A father is someone who acknowledges you as belonging to him, his flesh and blood. To some, this may not sound like such a grand gift, but for those who were orphans or grew up never having a father, it means everything.

I remember being so very young and how my little heart ached, and I longed to hear those words from my earthly father. I dreamed of having someone step forward and claim me as their daughter, declaring themselves to be my father. I so needed my father to step in and be my hero, scooping me up in his strong arms and assuring me that he loved me and that he wouldn't leave me again. I never experienced that as a child; only abandonment, shame, and the guilt that came from wondering why I wasn't wanted. But God had a different plan for my life because he didn't leave me as an orphan. He stepped up to Calvary and branded me as his own. I discovered a heavenly Father who was far greater, stronger, committed, faithful, and far more loving than any flesh and blood could ever be. God's promise to be a Father to us is monumental, but it comes with a calling, a calling to come out and be separate from the world. God, the Almighty, makes a promise to the woman who will dare to step forward and declare to the world unashamedly, "I belong to God." And when this declaration is heard, God unashamedly thunders his answer through the corridors of heaven, "And I belong to her!"

Only you can validate your heart for God because only you can give your heart away. No one can take it from you. Your heart is the one thing you have that is completely yours to give or keep as you choose; it's God's gift to you. But remember that deep within your heart is a place that only he can fill, and your heart will never be a home anywhere but with him. You must make the choice to give your heart completely to him by refusing to surrender it to anyone or anything else. You have been entrusted with the responsibility of guarding and keeping watch over it with all diligence, keeping it pure and holy. How the Father searches for such a heart, a heart in waiting. He explores the depths and heights of his vast earth finding no rest until that heart is found, the heart keeping itself only unto him, waiting in purity.

Spanning the scriptures are men and women who became the captives of the Living God by securing their hearts before him with reverence and worship. These same men and women were used by God to bring down kingdoms, wage war with the valiant, stand as judge before the nations, prophesy the future, shut up the skies for days and command the rain, part the raging waters of the sea, raise the dead and shake the foundations of hell. Why? All because they knew they belonged to another, one who is higher, greater, holy and worthy of all they are or ever hoped to be. They feared sin because they loved and respected their God. No sin was counted as small in their eyes because every sin grieves the heart of God.

As you contemplate your life in light of the truths penned upon these pages, I pray your eyes will be enlightened and that you will know what the hope of his calling for you is. I lay down my pen and bow the knee before our heavenly Father, from whom every family on earth derives their name, and plead for you, beloved daughter of God. I pause in holy awe before the one who formed your heart, fashioning you in his own likeness— like Father, like daughter. I asked, not for my sake, but for yours, that he would pour out great conviction of personal sins found within your life. I implore him to loosen all that fetters you to the world, every sin, to be brought to the surface of your mind and made clear before your eyes. And then without apology, I beg of him that he would give you no rest until you have made confession of every one and repented wholly of each.

God will withdraw his hand of favor from your life unless you deal thoroughly with every sin present in your life. Maybe you have jealousy, an unkind tongue, a haughty spirit, a judgmental heart, a criticizing attitude, gossip, fear, worry, dishonesty, unforgiveness, bitterness, laziness, or self righteousness. You may struggle with self absorbency, vanity, a works mentality, pleasing people, or a love for material things. You might be demanding or controlling, not wanting to let go because it means you might have to trust in another or not get your way. Complacency and legalism are often silent bandits that are hard to recognize in our own lives, but we seem to spot them clearly in another's. We usually have 20/20 vision when it comes to the wrong doings of others. We can spot it a mile away, can't we?

The sin list above is certainly not exhaustive, but it speaks volumes to the truth that sin can wear many different hats. We must recognize which hats we are wearing and bring them to God by removing them from our lives. So the question remains, what kind of woman do you want to be? What kind of woman are you? Do you have a fear of sin before your eyes or have you become desensitized to it? Do you view some sins as less destructive than others? Do you confess your sins daily seeking God's forgiveness so you can have continual dialogue with him? This is my prayer for you and for me.

We are women, God's great design, and he has a marvelous plan for each of us and that plan includes him using you and me for his kingdom. The Apostle Paul wrote my life's anthem, my life verse in Acts 20:24, and I want to share it with you, "For I do not consider my life of any account as dear to myself in order that I may finish my course, and the ministry which I received from the Lord Jesus, to testify solemnly of the gospel of the grace of God." You are his daughter, his beloved one, redeemed from the ashes of the earth. You are his and he is fully yours. What love the Father has for you and oh, the magnitude of his plans for your life. He has canvassed your life with rare beauty, and he waits to unveil it when the time is most perfect to his holy will. You are his masterpiece created for good works.

God loved each and every one of us before our life ever began. Our names were upon His lips, and engraved upon the heart of Holiness was the purpose our days upon the earth would fill. There has never been a break, a hesitation, or skip in the heartbeat of God's love for us. Even in our darkest hour of rebellion or lowest ebb of sin, the love of God has been steadfast, unshakable, and unrelenting. We are wholly His, and He will never lose the cords of His embrace upon our soul. There has never been a day, a moment, or span of time in our life's history line when God was not loving us! God has given to us the whole of His heart and affections. The enfold of His embrace will not surrender us!

If we desire to be the woman God will use, then it begins here—at the place of holiness, confessing and repenting of every sin. We must not view sin lightly nor allow its presence in our lives. It is not our duty or lot in life to point out the sins of others or heaven forbid we pass judgment upon them. We are equipped with an itinerary of our own sins that is large enough to keep us busy for the rest of our days. The log in our own eye is burdensome enough and vastly troublesome for us without trying to remove the speck in our sister's eye. We must turn our scrutinizing eye inward to the heart that God gave us responsibility and authority over. And under the God given care of choice, may we tremble at the thought of sin entering there in. Time is ticking away for eternity and every minute spent harboring sin in our lives is time we might as well have never been given at all. Precious moments packed full of eternal promise passing by the windows of our days never to pass by again.

We have this moment before us, to hold in our hand and choose what we will do with the truths brought before us. I asked you to pause with reverence before God and ask him to search the depths of your heart and surface every speck of ungodliness, every fiber that doesn't belong wholly to him. As it surfaces, I encourage you to write it down in the space provided for you. Take this list when you are finished and lay it at the feet of Jesus asking him to take it from you and to cleanse you from all unrighteousness. Confess your desire to be pleasing to him in every respect and then worship him for the Savior that he is. He is willing, able, and wanting to pour out his blessing in full upon every area of your life, but he's waiting on you. What will you do with the life God has given to you? What will you do with the sin you have given to yourself?

My Confession:

_____

_____

_____

_____

_____

_____

_____

_____

_____

_____

A Woman of Prayer

The earnest prayer of a righteous person has great power and produces wonderful results.

—James 5:16 (NLT)

Just as our heart longs for God himself, the deepest part of us calling out to the deepest part of him, it longs to commune with him. It has been this way from the beginning of time as we know it. Genesis 3:8 gives us a glimpse of this as it says, "And they heard the voice of the Lord God walking in the garden in the cool of the day…" When the dust of the day was settling upon the garden, God came down that he might walk with Adam and Eve in their world, step where their feet had trod and speak with them one on one about their day. His heart was to express his thoughts to them and allow them to express theirs. It's always been God's heart to have open dialogue with us every day. He intentionally fostered intimacy with his children, so they would long to keep him close. Prayer has been his design from the very beginning—him speaking his love to us and hearing our love spoken to him. His perfect will is to fellowship with us where we are, in our garden, in the land where he placed us to labor and live for him. Prayer is the fulfillment of his heart's greatest desire; to commune with you, the love of his heart, every day we live.

Volumes have been written, no doubt, on prayer. Upon their pages, the urgent message arises for the church of God to pray, to seek the face of the Lord. These faithful writers have discovered this message upon the eternal pages of the Bible. It's the constant call of heaven for every Christian to take up spiritual arms and pray. Though it is constant, it's often the most neglected. Woven through the pages of Holy Scripture is the urging to pray, the power of praying, and a faithful God who answers every prayer offered by a believing heart. Prayer is clearly revealed as God's urgent will for every child of his. Yet it is still clothed in holy wonder, veiled for those eyes who have yet to look heavenward for anything and everything. It's been said, "One should never initiate anything that he cannot saturate with prayer." Sidlow Baxter said, "Men may spurn our appeals, reject our message, oppose our arguments, despise our persons, but they are helpless against our prayers." A woman is never more powerful than when she is on her knees before God in holy communion seeking his face no matter the cost. No sweeter life will she find than that of unbroken dialogue with him— living, thinking, breathing, working, and ministering out loud to him and for him.

The prophet Elijah prayed to God upon Mt. Carmel, and God answered by sending down fire from heaven. When God was ready to bring Elijah to heaven, he sent forth his fiery chariot to escort him upward. Moses prayed for God to show him his glory and God did something he had never done nor has done since—he allowed Moses's eyes to look upon him from the back as he was passing by. God answered Hannah's prayers by giving her a son out of her barrenness. The early church prayed for Peter to be freed, and God sent an angel to deliver him. The prophet Daniel spent his entire ministry in prayer, and no man has ever been given the revelations of the coming Messiah as he. He prayed and God shut the mouths of lions. He enlightened kings, he was rescued from death, he interpreted dreams, and he stood in the presence of angels. Abraham prayed for his nephew Lot to be saved from the coming destruction of Sodom and Gomorrah. There's Isaiah, Gideon, Joshua, Jeremiah, Shaddrach, Meshach, and Abednego, who touched heaven in prayer. Samson prayed for his strength to return and slew more men in his death than he did in life. We must not fail to mention King David, Solomon, or Deborah.

Upon the written pages of history, we found a man by the name of Charles Finney down on his knees crying out in earnest prayer for God to save the lost. His prayers were heard in heaven and the whole country was shaken for God. We read of John Wesley who was devoted to prayer, and ten thousand souls were converted to Christ. It is said of Wesley that he prayed at least three hours every day. There's George Mueller, a man full of faith in the power of God. He took every need he had straight to God in prayer and because of it, a multitude of orphans never missed a meal. Clinging to God's promise of Psalm 34:10, "The young lions do lack and suffer hunger; but they who seek the Lord shall not be in want of any good thing," Mueller refused to let go until provision was given. Prayer was not only his lifeline but also that of the orphans placed in his care. He once told a man that in his fifty years of prayer, he had never failed to have an audience with the King.

Dwight Moody rose long before the sun came up in order to seek God in prayer. He was a man desperate for God's favor, his power, his provision, and salvation of the lost. His prayers are still impacting lives today. The list would go on and on of faithful Christians who dared to bombard the gates of heaven for a moving of God upon their generation, their country, and their personal lives. God does answer prayer, beloved, and because of it the world is changed and he is glorified. It's not our methods, our plans, our talents, or even our ministries that will change lives and impact the world for God's glory; it's our prayers. God can take every minute of our praying and pour into eternity. He takes the prayers offered in faith and transforms them into realities far beyond anything we could imagine.

Charles Spurgeon was a man of prayer. A story taken from the *Our Daily Bread* gives us the following account taken from his life: "Five young college students were spending a Sunday in London, so they went to hear the famed C.H. Spurgeon preach. While waiting for the doors to open, the students were greeted by a man who asked, 'Gentlemen, let me show you around. Would you like to see the heating plant of this church?' They were not particularly interested, for it was a hot day in July. But they didn't want to offend the stranger, so they consented. The young men were taken down a stairway, a door was quietly opened, and their guide whispered, 'This is our heating plant.' Surprised, the students saw

700 people bowed in prayer, seeking a blessing on the service that was soon to begin in the auditorium above. Softly closing the door, the gentleman then introduced himself. It was none other than Charles Spurgeon." (Our Daily Bread, April 24, *The Sunday Boiler Room*).

Spurgeon knew that prayer could do anything God could do. Psalm 105:4 declares, "Seek the Lord and His strength; seek His face continually." He understood that speaking with such an awesome, powerful, life-giving God was not a casual encounter. It's a privilege not to take lightly or take for granted. Our attitude toward prayer is a direct reflection of our opinion of God. How often do we neglect it, misuse it, and refuse it? Until we recognize prayer is not only for giving life to our spiritual walk, but that it is the life, it will never become a priority for us. I'm not speaking of corporate prayer, although it is a vital necessity and command of God for the church, but rather I'm speaking of personal prayer. Corporate prayer is simply an overflow of our personal prayer time with God. Our personal communing with God will be the life flow of every other area of our life and ministry within the body of Christ. We will never impact God's world until we impact his throne room.

Those who have left the deepest imprints upon the timeline of history have been men and women of prayer. The impressions left upon their generation have stretched forth their hand of influence leaving their mark even upon our own lives. Praying people speak marvelous faith into future generations through their intercession. Prayer not only has the power to move God, it has the power to move people. It is a mighty force upon the earth changing history, moving history in the direction of God himself. As Christians, I believe we all desire to be used by God and see his power demonstrated through and in our lives. But apart from prayer this will not happen. Prayer is the self-sacrificing link that connects earth and heaven. Prayer binds them in holy union that the will of God might be carried out through earthen vessels. What a marvelous mystery, the reach and influence prayer has upon God's earth.

We can be used by God to save souls around the world without ever leaving our home. Prayer is not contingent upon its birth place but rather upon its resting place. That bears repeating, "Prayer is not contingent upon its birth place but rather upon its resting place!" Jonah prayed from the belly of the whale. Moses prayed from the deadness of the wilderness. Paul prayed with blinded eyes and he and Silas prayed from a prison cell. Job prayed from ashes. Gideon prayed from a winepress, and Jesus prayed from the cross. David prayed from the valley of sin, and Noah prayed from the ark. All were heard, not because of where their prayer was offered or the dignity of them, but from the lodging place the prayer came to rest upon—the throne of Father in heaven.

These prayers were not recognized for their length or their words, but for the heart offering them. Just like the thief hanging next to Jesus who simply prayed, "Lord, remember me." He was a man who recognized his sin, giving no excuse only a confession that he wanted Jesus. His heart prayed with such humility from the agony of his life and from his utter helplessness. He didn't know what else to do. In his weakness, he cried out to the only hope he had who was Jesus. W.S. Bounds said, "Prayer is weakness leaning upon omnipotence." Prayer from a desperate heart, believing that God is their only source, rises before him taking a place of importance in his presence. All of these believed in and depended upon prayer. How much have we not received simply because we would not pray?

Do you depend upon prayer? Is prayer the staple of your Christian walk? Just like the thief who was honored to hang next to the very Son of God, his Savior, we must seize the opportunities God gives to us. Isaiah 55:6 says, "Seek the Lord while He may be found; Call upon Him while He is near." The thief is a living example of this truth for us. God had brought Jesus near to him that day in the midst of his suffering, upon his death bed. We can cry out in our lowest, most defiled state, even upon our death bed, and Jesus will not turn us away. This is the power of prayer that even upon our crosses of suffering, we can draw near to him. Prayer brought salvation to a lost soul in his most desperate hour. The consequences he would have endured for all eternity were cancelled out because of his willingness to recognize his need for salvation. God longs for us to embrace prayer, to understand the magnitude of its importance. Jesus spoke of it in Luke 18. Read his words with me.

> Then Jesus told his disciples a parable to show
> them that they should always pray and not give
> up. He said, "In a certain town there was a judge
> who neither feared God nor cared about men.

And there was a widow in that town who kept coming to him with the plea, 'Grant me justice against my adversary.' For some time he refused. But finally he said to himself, 'Even though I don't fear God or care about men, yet because this widow keeps bothering me, I will see that she gets justice, so that she won't eventually wear me out with her coming!' And the Lord said, 'Listen to what the unjust judge says. And will not God bring about justice for his chosen ones, who cry out to him day and night? Will he keep putting them off? I tell you, he will see that they get justice, and quickly. However, when the Son of Man comes, will he find faith on the earth?'"

—Luke 18:1–8 (NIV)

Jesus had just finished speaking of his second coming and he immediately, with great purpose, begins to speak of the urgency to pray at all times and not faint nor lose heart. He confronts his listeners and all who would one day read his words with an inevitable choosing we must make. We must choose to pray or lose heart and faint. It's one choice or the other. We have the privilege of crying out to the unseen Sovereign in the heavens who is ever waiting for us to call to him, or we can choose to lose heart and faint in the midst of our lives. Those without prayer will live in the shadow of failure, susceptible to fainting within looming over them, waiting to overtake them. Prayer is the combat and the protector of the heart according to Jesus. Prayer is to the heart what a shepherd is to his sheep.

Prayer protects, defends, strengthens, encourages, and bombards the heart with the presence of God, ushering in fullness of hope. It moves the Father to act on our behalf.

We have in our generation, more than in any other in human history, a people who have been reared apart from the love and reality of a heavenly Father. Our generation lives, for the most part, as orphans among the other lost orphans, all groping to find real life, true joy, and purpose for living. Their voices raise up in pessimism against faith and trust in God, speaking forth words of despair from the emptiness of their own heart—empty hearts that long to be held, rescued, filled, validated, and renewed lack the answer because they are crying out against God rather than to God. This is the sound of lostness, beloved, and it fills the air. It surrounds us at every turn filling and seizing all who will listen to its meaningless words and empty philosophies. Their hearts are hardened like stone and their ears are dull of hearing. Jesus gives us the reality that we will all faint or we will pray. We will end up like the masses, unless we dedicate our very lives to prayer.

The Apostle Paul wrote:

> Wherefore I desire that ye faint not at my tribulations for you, which is your glory. For this cause I bow my knees unto the Father of our Lord Jesus Christ, Of whom the whole family in heaven and earth is named, that He would grant you, according to the riches of his glory, to be strengthened with might by his Spirit in the inner man; That Christ may dwell

in your hearts by faith; that ye, being rooted and grounded in love, may be able to comprehend with all saints what is the breadth, and length, and depth, and height; And to know the love of Christ, which surpasses knowledge, that ye might be filled with all the fullness of God. Now unto him that is able to do exceeding abundantly above all that we ask or think, according to the power that worketh in us, unto Him be glory in the church by Christ Jesus throughout all ages, world without end. Amen.

—Ephesians 3:13–21 (KJV)

Paul tells the church of Ephesus that there is a "power that worketh in them," but what power? Listen to his words precious one, "For this cause I bow my knee unto the Father of our Lord Jesus Christ, of whom the whole family in heaven and earth is named, that he would grant you…" And he goes on with great confidence listing out his petition for them before the throne of God. And in the end, he goes on to give credit where credit is due, "Now unto Him that is able to do exceeding abundantly above all that we ask or think, according to the power that worketh in us…" Paul takes a spotlight and shines it upon prayer, but not just any prayer—prayer that is offered through bended knee to the one true Living God. This prayer accomplishes much; it opens up the flood gates of heaven's resources and washes over our lives. The great apostle was absolutely, without wavering, confident in one thing— prayer. He knew who he was praying to and that he was faithful and unfailing. Jesus ended his discourse on prayer with a "dagger to the heart" question for every one of us, "Nevertheless, when the Son of man comes, will He find faith on earth?" (Luke 18:8b, RSV).

Jesus makes no apologies and leaves no room for doubt that he is coming again and *when* he comes, what kind of faith will he find upon the earth? Will he find his daughter praying because she has placed her faith and trust in him and in him alone? Or will he find his beloved sleeping, going the way of the world, living in ease, or struggling to make her on way in life? How many countless times have I tried in my own strength to fix my situation without even a thought at looking to God? It has happened more times than I would want to admit. Prayer is work, it takes time, it's a struggle for power, and yes, a great struggle for power. I believe this is where a lot of us in the church miss it. We are not willing to surrender our circumstances, our children, jobs, homes, marriages, finances, hurts, health, or our very lives into the loving hands of God. We don't want to wave our rights over our lives, so we don't pray as we should. It's a struggle for power just as much as it is a struggle for faith.

This struggle will never pass until we choose to believe that we can and should trust God. Trust is giving to God what is already his without expecting anything in return. There is no shadow of turning with him. He has always been, and he is and will forever be. We belong fully and absolutely wholly to him. He is able, he is willing, and he is waiting for us to run to him, yielding into his mighty arms of power and unfailing providence. He will do what he says, he will do, and he will never stop loving us. We are his children and he waits—longs to walk in the cool of the garden and there commune with us all the evening long. It's holy fellowship with God apart from which we will never know fullness of joy. It is his gift to us and our life line to him.

So great is this matchless gift to us that Philippians 4:6–7 tells us, "Be anxious for nothing, but in everything, by prayer and supplication let your requests be made known to God. And the peace of God, which surpasses all understanding, will guard your hearts and minds in Christ Jesus." Prayer is our lifeline because it is our funnel of peace from heaven to earth. When we are anxious, fearful, and confused, prayer will settle us. It will calm our fears, taking every anxious thought captive and bringing it to God. And his peace, which will pass anything we could ever even begin to explain, will set up a watch over our heart and mind. God's peace is our protector, and we receive his peace through the line of prayer. Anytime we are stricken with worry and panic, prayer is the only answer. Prayer is thanking rather than complaining; it is believing that anything is possible with God. Prayer secures our hope and anchors us in the deepness of all God is.

It's easier to talk about God than to God. Prayer involves denial of self and everything that we could be doing instead. It takes us laying down our selfishness, our tiredness, knowing he is enough; and our busyness, believing that he is worthy. We must realize that prayer is an absolute, vital necessity in our relationship with God. Our failure to realize this truth is what keeps us from the deeper walk, the intimacy with holiness, and hinders our eyes from seeing his glory displayed. He wants this for every one of his children. This is why Jesus asked the "dagger question": When he comes will he find you to be a praying woman? Will he discover you locked away in your secret place loving him with your time, honoring him with your trust, and embracing him through your prayers? Will he see you upon your knees interceding for his children, for his world that he loves so very much? Will he find you pouring out your very life at the feet of his Father, lavishing your praise upon him? How will he find you, precious daughter of God?

From one woman to another, I want to plead with you with all earnestness my heart and flesh can muster and say, "Pray, pray, pray and then pray some more". Pray as if there was no tomorrow. Pray as if your life depended upon it, as if the Lord were returning tomorrow at sunrise. Pray knowing that God is waiting, anticipating your cry, listening for your cry to ascend to his holy hill. What keeps you from praying? What drives you to pray? God is pleased when we run to him in our seasons of distress, but he loves it when we run to him simply because we have missed him, and we long to be in his presence. Have you ever missed the presence of God? Do you know that he misses yours always?

I leave you with this challenge, this calling, "Pray without ceasing" (1 Thessalonians 5:17). Until you identify what interrupts your unceasing prayers, you will float along at the bidding of the waters of self, and you will find in the end your life could have been so much more. God will limit his use of you until you decide with bold abandon to pray without ceasing, to live to pray. He uses a woman who prays not for selfish gain, not for self glory, not to have her own plans fulfilled, but the one who prays to the Father, "Thy will be done on earth as it is in heaven. Whatever is loosed on earth will be loosed in heaven." What will you choose to loose in prayer upon the earth that will be loosed in heaven? It begins with a heart to pray. Begin to pray and you will find that he will cultivate a heart to pray within you until you find you can do nothing less. This is where true living begins for his kingdom. The rise and fall of many ministries, and many called individuals have revolved around prayer, or the lack of.

If God were to pen every time we should have prayed and did not, what would the scroll of his will show? How much have we lost because we would not pray? How many souls could we have reached for Christ if only we would have given time to pray? Where would we be now if we had committed ourselves to earnest prayer twenty years ago? How much more would God have done in, and through us, if we would have been a praying woman? How many sleepless nights could we have missed, how many relationships rescued, sins refused, fears overcome, forgiveness poured out, and a bold witness given if only we had prayed? Hear him now, my sweet friend, hear him calling to your heart, beckoning you to draw nigh to him, to walk and commune. He's always waiting for you. Won't you come? Give him your all and he will become your everything.

I am not the woman of prayer that I long to be, but I'm striving, yearning, and leaning into him that he might lean into me. I confess my need to pray more, worry less, and release more of those things I cling so tightly too. I have far more failures than I will ever have successes. But one thing I have learned is that I need God always. I can do nothing apart from him. He is my everything and I'm desperate for more of him, all of him. I have set my course to be the woman of prayer that he longs for me to be, and I will not surrender myself to things that have no eternal value. I pray you will join me, beloved. Let's raise our voices as one unto the glory of God and feel the darkness tremble.

Let's close out this chapter by writing out our heart's cry to God in prayer. Talk to him and share your thoughts with him. Confess your failures and express your heart's desire to him. Pray to him and love him now with your words.

My Prayer To God:

_____

_____

_____

_____

_____

_____

_____

_____

_____

_____

The Garments of Humility

All of you clothe yourselves with humility toward one another, for God is opposed to the proud, but gives grace to the humble.

—1 Peter 5:5

There's nothing more important to a bride than her wedding gown. One of my most treasured moments was the day I saw my daughters in their wedding gowns. Like so many mothers, it's such a bitter sweet time to walk through with them. These prized moments we were privileged to share, radiated with joy and the thrill of walking down the aisle to marry the love of their life permeated every thought, every decision made. That day, they had but one person in mind, just one consuming dream, their beloved groom. In my mind's eye, I can, even now, see them walking out clothed with the garments of promise and hope. Both girls were heart-stopping, so absolutely stunning that they took my breath away. Their adornment transformed them from young girls to women right before my eyes.

I have two wonderful daughters who are as beautiful on the inside as they are on the outside. Their wedding garments lit up the beauty veiled within captivating not only their mother's attention, but everyone in the room. It was their adornment that seized the platform of attention. The moment washed over my heart with such joy as I saw their outward glory do justice to their inward splendor. It is a beautiful thing when our adornment honors the heart it cloaks. The bride's adornment is timeless for her groom, and he will always remember the day that he saw her clothed in beauty, walking down the aisle where he was waiting. His heart has waited for this day—waited to hear the love of his life declare her eternal love for him. She's coming to surrender herself only and fully to him, the one who loves her. She yields her rights, all committing her life to his. It's this purpose that beautifies the adornment that fills the room with the warmth and glow of eternal love being brought together. The beauty of the bride's reverent humility is all together lovely in the eyes of God.

Just as the garments of white illumine the beloved bride of man, so the garments of humility illumine the bride of the Lord. Humility means meekness or gentleness. There's nothing more lovely than a gracious woman who is clothed in the sweet raiment of humility. She catches the eye of God. In fact, he is drawn to her. Listen to what he says in Isaiah 66:2, "But to this one I will look, to the one who is humble and contrite of spirit…" He is ever in search of the heart that is humble. Once found, he moves without reservation to immediately secure, strengthen, adorn, and applaud her life with his manifold, love, and favor. She is a rare jewel not hewn from the shadows of the earth, but rather from the light found only in Jesus. This woman has caught a glimpse of eternity. She looks beyond the things of the world and leaning in to him; she reaches; she extends all of herself with every ounce of her will to lay hold of him who first laid hold of her (Philippians 3:12).

She refuses to settle, refuses acknowledgement, and absolutely stands against anything that would rob God of his glory—of his rightful place. She remembers that the applause of man is but fading shadows among the earth, which will come to ruin in the end. She seeks not to be found in the glow of fleshly recognition, but beneath the cloud of his Shekinah Glory. It takes purpose of heart to acknowledge God in all things; to submit one's self, one's work and ministry underneath the canopy of his glorious wonder. The wise will understand the life of flesh—that it is but a vapor and then vanishes as quickly as it came. Listen to the words of James, "Yet you do not know what your life will be like tomorrow. You are just a vapor that appears for a little while and then vanishes away" (James 4:14); vapor has no substance. We cannot grasp it in our hands and contain it. So it is with life. Anything that comes from the flesh, our works, accomplishments, awards, degrees, etc. are only temporary; they will pass away when we die. We do not belong to the things of the earth and the earth does not belong to us.

We need heroes of humility upon the earth to remind us of the validity of this truth. Valiant humility is in danger of becoming extinct. The book of Numbers 12:3 reveals such a hero, "Now the man Moses was very humble, more than any man who was on the face of the earth." Moses understood the reality of his weakness. Listen to his prayer which sheds great light for us upon his humility:

> A Prayer of Moses, the man of God. Lord, You have been our dwelling place in all generations.

Before the mountains were born Or You gave birth to the earth and the world, Even from everlasting to everlasting, You are God. You turn man back into dust And say, "Return, O children of men." For a thousand years in Your sight Are like yesterday when it passes by, Or as a watch in the night. You have swept them away like a flood, they fall asleep; in the morning they are like grass which sprouts anew. In the morning it flourishes and sprouts anew; toward evening it fades and withers away.

—Psalm 90:1–6

Moses's humility was recognized by God in a way that no ordinary man had ever received. Exodus 33:11 tells us that God spoke with Moses face to face, just as a man speaks to his friend. He was a vessel of humility and because of it, God poured into the vessel and sat it before him to polish it with shine of his glory. The greatest leaders in God's hall of fame are not the strong but those who first became weak and humbled before him. If you are a strong woman in your eyes, then God will pass you over for intimacy with him. Acknowledging our weaknesses and the temporary days of earth and blood is the first step to stripping away pride. Until we make much to do about God and nothing to do about us, pride will continue to rob you of God's best. Moses goes on to say in verse 10 of this same passage of Psalms, "As for the days of our life, they contain seventy years, or if due to strength, eighty years, yet their pride is but labor and sorrow; For soon it is gone and we fly away" (Psalm 90:10).

Moses refused to see himself as anything more than a man of flesh and blood created by a God who is infinitely wise and all powerful—holy yet personal. He refused the high road and embraced the low road because knowing the secret of God's glory canopies over the seemingly insignificant, the outcast and even the forgotten ones. It's found in the valleys, the lowlands, and in difficult passages; it's following God through the desserts of life, not through the land of luxury and ease. Moses never saw himself as more than just a man. What made his life significant was God choosing him out of all the other men upon the face of the earth to do his bidding. God speaks very highly of Moses when he says,

> Then the Lord came down in a pillar of cloud and stood at the doorway of the tent, and He called Aaron and Miriam. When they had both come forward, He said, "Hear now My words: If there is a prophet among you, I, the Lord, shall make Myself known to him in a vision. I shall speak with him in a dream. Not so, with My servant Moses, He is faithful in all My household; With him I speak mouth to mouth, Even openly, and not in dark sayings, And he beholds the form of the Lord. Why then were you not afraid to speak against My servant, against Moses?" So the anger of the Lord burned against them and He departed.
>
> —Numbers 12:5–9

Why does God do this for his humble servant? James 4:10 tells us why, "Humble yourself in the presence of

God and He will exalt you." This is what he did with Moses. It's the golden rule of heaven for the humble heart. Humility burns a path of beauty for honor to follow. It's God who gives value to our lives. The seal of his affection upon us is simply by his choosing not our merits. Moses saw his own frailty in the light of God's power. He understood how ordinary he was in the presence of the extraordinary God with whom we have to do. Moses never lowered God to the dust of the earth from whence man was drawn but rather he raised him up to the highest place of honor resting above every other name. Do you want God to use you? Then humility must be your adornment in ministry. Nothing less will do for the woman whom God will use. And for this humble woman are the mighty promises of God held in unfailing faithfulness ready to be poured out upon her.

Humility is an anchor of the promises of God. Listen to just a few, "O Lord, You have heard the desire of the humble; You will strengthen their heart, You will incline Your ear" (Psalm 10:17). The humble woman has an unlimited source of strength for her heart and the audience of God when she prays. Can you just stop and say, "Wow, thank you, Lord!" This wonderful word *strengthen*, as used in this verse, means "to make stable, to firmly establish, to secure, to prepare, provide, to fix, to settle, to be restored and cause to endure." How many times have you needed stability? Does your heart long to be held, secured because life has overwhelmed you? Maybe you've needed restoration or the ability to endure through a painful season of life. For all of these needs, the humble woman of God will not lack provision.

Never underestimate the hidden power of a humble woman. Although humble, God pours out his provision infusing her heart with strength, and when the heart of a woman is strong, she is beautifully resilient. The Apostle Paul said, "When I am weak, then I am strong" (2 Corinthians 12:10). What an inheritance that humility leaves for us. We long to be strong, and we wonder why so many others seem to sail through the storms of life without fear and full of peace. God waits for us to come to him in absolute humility, in total dependence upon him. We must deplete all of our own strength and allow God to fill us with his. The pouring out of the self-strong woman is what God waits patiently for. He looks for bravery in a heart that is vulnerable enough to confess her weakness and her desperation for God's help. She knows she won't make it without him and when he pours into her, she knows without hesitation that it's all of him. The woman who has come face to face with her weakness, will find herself face to face with the power of an everlasting Father.

As a woman, our hearts are vulnerably drawn to acceptance, security, and most of all love. Therefore, we easily lend our affections to people, our dreams to the world, and find that they lead us not to what we were in search of, but regrettably to pain, brokenness and scars. The promise of his provision comes because of the humility found within the suffering, not in the suffering itself. This principal of truth is often the timeline for our suffering. Andrew Murray wrote, "Pride must die in you, or nothing of heaven can live in you." Humility is preceded by the funeral of pride. Before, humility comes a breaking down of heart, bending low into the dust before God, forsaking one's sin and crying out for his forgiveness. Humility recognizes the hand of an omnipotent God, who works his might through them and that they are just a conduit of his greatness. When this takes place, we gain a fresh impulse for heaven, and awakening of new beginnings with God, having a sense of our weakness colliding with his strength. This is the crux of humility: recognizing that it is God who does, has done, and is doing the work through us.

Let me share a prayer with you that is befitting of our topic:

Prayer of an Anonymous Abbess,

Lord, thou knowest better than myself that I am growing older and will soon be old. Keep me from becoming too talkative, and especially from the unfortunate habit of thinking that I must say something on every subject and at every opportunity.

Release me from the idea that I must straighten out other people's affairs. With my immense treasure of experience and wisdom, it seems a pity not to let everybody partake of it. But thou knowest, Lord, that in the end I will need a few friends.

Keep me from the recital of endless details; give me wings to get to the point.

Grant me the patience to listen to the complaints of others; help me to endure them with charity. But seal my lips on my own aches and pains—they increase with the increasing years and my inclination to recount them is also increasing.

I will not ask thee for improved memory, only for a little more humility and less self-assurance when my own memory doesn't agree with that of others. Teach me the glorious lesson that occasionally I may be wrong.

Keep me reasonably gentle. I do not have the ambition to become a saint—it is so hard to live with some of them—but a harsh old person is one of the devil's masterpieces.

Make me sympathetic without being sentimental, helpful but not bossy. Let me discover merits where I had not expected them and talents in people whom I had not thought to possess any. And, Lord, give me the grace to tell them so.

Amen

—Unknown

The humble woman is gentle, kind, and judging another is not in her demeanor simply because she has come face to face with her own weaknesses. This is why you will never find a humble woman partaking of a conversation that speaks negatively of another. Humility will not endorse or condone speech that is unbecoming to its nature. And it will never bring low another through words or actions because they know the greatness of their own shortcomings. Her words are not loud and boisterous but rather they are laced with grace and tender mercies. She is never threatened at the success of another because her security is anchored in the humble position she has found in the salvation of the Lord. Death of our own fame must take place in our heart before humility can be birthed within us. Sometimes the fame of self dies slowly, unwilling to let go of the glory it yearns to possess for itself. The charm of the world and its recognition must be broken—shattered from our midst. The greatest test for any woman or man of God is the recognition test—the humility scale. Secret yearnings for applause will surface eventually, and a false humility will be discovered. God longs for genuine, gut level, endlessly merciful meekness in his child. To fulfill this longing, he will circumstance our life into such a way that we become teachable, pliable for his working. The school of his learning often carries with it a forced enrollment of students! It's not a place we run to with joy and excitement. We are usually thrown into it by an overwhelming situation, finding ourselves in very painful place. We can either struggle in our self-pity and fight against the providence of God, or we can yield ourselves to his way, his will, his every touch upon us. Like a mineworker digging in the dark of the deepness of the earth to hewn out a precious jewel, so the Master Miner will unearth a priceless treasure in you. He is steady and as sure as the sun rising in his performing his work in you. He is stripping away layer upon layer of the unlovely until all that is left is the radiance of humility. "For I am confident of this very thing, that He who began a good work in you will perfect it until the day of Christ Jesus" (Philippians 1:6).

I have known the deepness of his touch upon my life as he continues to strip away all of me that more of him may be seen. God uses people as the refining flames to turn the heat up in our lives, smoking the dross of self out, so it can be dealt with. One such time in my life where I found myself having to leave the church I had been in for over twenty years. I was still very young in my understanding of a lot of things and so this was devastating for me. A new pastor had come in because the only pastor I had ever known as a Christian had left to go serve God in the mission fields. My safety net had been pulled out from under me, and my spirit was under attack. Hurtful things were being said; you know how the tongue is—it loves a stink! I called a dear godly friend of mine to pour out my sorrows like an ocean, hoping for a wave of compassionate understanding. In layman terms, I wanted to invite her to my pity party. As I told of my sorrows and painful situation, describing all the horrible things that were being said of me; she had but one reply to give me, "Whatever anyone thinks or says of you, it's better than what you really are apart from Jesus."

The prideful woman will never find the counsel of the humble easy to swallow. She was at that time and is today one of the most humble women I've ever known. Her humility spoke precious volumes into my life at a time that I desperately needed to see that God was trying to strip me of the pride that had burrowed its way so deeply into my life. I was broken at the thought of it, and I almost didn't receive what the Lord wanted me to hear because of the hidden arrogance within me. I was sinfully prideful and yet was completely blind to it. God stripped the veil from my eyes that I might behold myself in the mirror of hard truth, but it was his truth. But when I saw it, when I finally got it and confessed the shame of it before the Lord, peace began to fall. Bitterness and hurt withdrew from the lodging place I had buried it. Proverbs 22:4 became a living truth in my life, "The reward of the humility and the fear of the Lord are riches, honor, and life".

Honor came in God's time but little tastes at a time. The difference was this time, I didn't want any honor, only for him to have all the glory and praise. It was no longer about the work of the Lord but rather it was now about the Lord of the work. My walk with him became more intimate, more dependent, and more meaningful. He was my focus, not people, not even the work of ministry. I saw myself as I was, before a Holy God. I was and am a most wretched soul apart from him. I understood mercy at a deeper level. It was truly God's gift to me, although at first I did not view it as such. I thought surely God would need a rest from me for a while. Yet after the painful dust settled and I was rested in who I was in him, he began the journey of going deeper still—more loss, more pain, but more glory.

I am still somewhat naive to a lot of things and especially so at that point in life, but one pervading reality still hits me hard: The more God blesses me, the fewer friends in church seem to rejoice. But the more God takes from me, what joy it seems to bring them. I remember the day the Lord led my study to this scripture for the first time, "My soul will make its boast in the Lord; the humble will hear it and rejoice" (Psalm 34:2). In ministry, you are vulnerably transparent and your life is often an open book. Inevitably, you are the target for blame or unrealistic expectations, but you can also be the object of envy and make enemies you never knew you had. The psalmist had no doubt experienced this in his own life. When God uses you, blesses your ministry or life, the humble will hear it and rejoice. This is the true mark of humility.

There are different levels of loss and sorrow. With each new furrowed ground, new discoveries of self emerge. He is faithful to that work that he began, precious daughter of God. And so in this earthen vessel, now over thirty years of walking with him, the process goes on. He is still stripping away the worthless to give the eternal. But I must say that humble pie is an acquired taste! I know the loss of all things precious to me, from material things, to family, to health, to ministry, reputation, and even a marriage. Humility is the low road, and I have left my footprints upon its soil, tear stains along its path. But I have further to go, much further to go. But with steady eye and determined soul, I press on yearning for more of him to be seen and less of me. I have thrown myself utterly upon this prevailing promise, "You have also given me the shield of Your salvation, And Your right hand upholds me; And Your gentleness makes me great" (Psalm 18:35).

It's his gentleness or *humility* that makes us great. Let me leave you with a charge of truth woven together from the holy pages of God:

As one who has been chosen of God, holy and beloved, put on a heart of...humility (Colossians 3:12). Sanctify Christ as Lord in your heart, always ready to make a defense to everyone who asks you to give an account for the hope that is in you, yet with humility (I Peter 3:15). And when you are cast down, you will speak with confidence because the humble woman He will save (Job 22:29). And if, my daughter who is called by name will humble herself and pray seeking my face and turn from her sins then, I will hear her from heaven and I will forgive her of all her sin and bring healing to her life (2 Chronicles 7:14). Therefore, humble yourself under the mighty hand of God that He may exalt you at the proper time (1 Peter 5:6). And to sum up everything, every woman be harmonious, sympathetic, sisterly, kindhearted, and humble in spirit (1 Peter 3:8).

In the beginning God created the heavens and the earth. Now the earth was formless and empty, darkness was over the surface of the deep, and the Spirit of God was hovering over the waters. And God said, "Let there be light," and there was light. God saw that the light was good, and he separated the light from the darkness.

—Genesis 1:1-4 (NIV)

May you be found adorned in the splendor and manifold beauty of all that God is, radiantly holy and filled with his praises. I pray you will bow low before the Father, who has loved you, pursued you, and cherished you all the days of your life. Speak his praise and greatness before the throngs of the great congregations and raise a banner unto Jesus. Walk with fear and trembling cloaked in the unlimited strength of your God. Take time to journal your thoughts my sweet friend.

My Thoughts:

_____

_____

_____

_____

_____

_____

The Power of God's Word

In the beginning, God created the heavens and the earth. And the earth was formless and void, and darkness was over the surface of the deep; and the Spirit of God was moving over the surface of the waters. Then God said, 'let there be light'; and there was light."

—Genesis 1:1–2

In lone stillness, as a safeguard over the deepness of unknown darkness, no sound is heard, no words yet formed upon the tongue of man.

The Spirit of the Holy One is rising.

Winds have yet to take flight across the vastness of God's creation; no form of life rose from the dust.

The Ancient One is stirring, he begins to move.

There is no heartbeat echoing forth the song of life into the atmosphere. No mother's arms graced with the warmth of her new born babe. A baby's cry has yet to be released into the atmosphere of the universe...

A sound is heard...It's the heartbeat of the Elohim pulsating over the surface of nothingness as thunderous beauty held captive by time itself.

A song of praise unformed anticipates its freedom. There is no voice of adoration ascending from the lips of mankind; no melody penned by the hand of earthen vessels.

The Great I am, as thunderous beauty held captive by time itself, readies himself.

The choir of angels singing over the lost, who has finally come home have assembled themselves before the throne of the Creator, but there song is still unsung. They are longing, anticipating, waiting for word permitting them to break forth in singing.

The word finally comes, "Arise my love, ascend songs of life unto my holy hill and let the beauty of God fill the universe with his worship."

As Lazarus, entombed in the darkness of death, wrapped up in lifelessness, a word comes forth. It speaks into the darkness enveloped under the canopy of his power the words of life, "Let there be light." And there was light and life emerged and darkness fled from its countenance. The glorious voice of God commanded the elements according to his perfect will, for they could do nothing less than yield to his every desire. He is their master, the one forming, calling forth and summoning to perform his desire. Where there is life, there is light; and where there is light, there is life. God instructed the boundaries of life to culminate in the light, not in the darkness. Before he would stretch forth his omnipotent hand of creation, he birthed the light. When light is present, life can come forth. This is his way, his plan, and his design formed even before the foundations of the earth were set upon its pillars.

Although the darkness is under the watchful eye of God, under his control and movement, he established the light as his garden from which all other life would come forth. The first rule God founded in creation that we do well to remember is this: the darkness is under him, the light is from him. It is his gift to the world, he loves so very much. The life he intends to fill his earth comes from the light he called forth, never from the darkness. We know life in his light, we bear fruit in the light and we fill his earth in this light. The light was given first place in his world and it has never changed. If we are going to be life-giving women upon his earth, we begin here at the beginning with understanding of and surrender to his established blueprint. You will never be the woman God created you to be apart from living with the boundaries of his light he gave to the world.

There is a deepness of truth that we must learn to mine from in our spiritual and physical lives. As we venture further in the account of creation, we find that God moved to establish the authority of the light. It would govern the day and the night. Read with me Genesis 1:4–5,14:

> And God saw that the light was good; and God separated the light from the darkness. And God called the light day, and the darkness He called night. And there was evening and there was morning, one day. Then God said, "Let there be lights in the expanse of the heavens to separate

the day from the night, and let them be for
signs, and for seasons, and for days and years."

The first day was established by God in this ordained
boundary of the light. His light was to be separate from
the darkness and his light would rule over not only the
day, but also over the night, over the darkness. His
light was not only given boundaries, but it was given
authority over the darkness. The light was to "rule or
govern" the darkness and the day. How many of us live
outside the light during our days, and when the night
comes we don't know where to turn because our life
has no yield to the light? We were not brought forth in
the darkness but in light. Therefore, light is our origin
of life, our sustainer of life. If it is our origin of life in
the day, then all the more it is our source of life in the
times of darkness. This is the first rule of life for God's
children. Inscribe it upon the tablets of your heart and
upon the palms of your hand as a reminder that you,
precious one of God, belong to the day not to the night.

The Apostle John spoke these words, "And this is
the message we have heard from him and announce to
you, that God is light, and in Him there is no darkness
at all. If we say that we have fellowship with Him and
yet walk in the darkness, we lie and do not practice
the truth" (1 John 1:5–6). When he spoke and said let
there be light, he was speaking forth, breathing out
himself into his creation; he is light. He is not a source
of light, a form of light, a picture of light, he is light.
This is a truth we can't wrap the fullness of human
understanding around. Although, God is eternal, he

has always been and will always be, on this day he spoke himself into the world as the canvas upon which he would paint the beauty of his world. In essence, God was saying, "Let there be God in the world." God has always intended to be seen and known by his creation. It is the heartbeat of creation, the driving force behind everything else that followed.

The earnest heed of God's heart is to reveal himself in all things at all times. This is why he placed light even in the midst of the darkness he had separated, so there would be no place void of his presence. Even God did not curse the darkness but lit the candle of mercy in its firmament. The darkness cannot overpower the light, but the light can overtake the darkness. Mercy and justice are dictated in space as we understand that the darkness was not left as an orphan. An orphan has no father, no known creator, no authority, or accountability. The darkness has one who rules over its realm. It is not without accountability. The light governs its premises and exposes all that takes place within the tent of darkness.

God would never have created a world, his world, without him in it. He gave all life the gift of himself and for himself. Listen to the words found in James 1:17–18:

> Every good thing bestowed and every perfect gift is from above, coming down from the father of lights, with whom there is no variation, or shifting shadow. In the exercise of His will He brought us forth by the word of truth, so that

we might be, as it were the first fruits among
His creatures.

In the exercise of his perfect will, he put himself
before all things. Before the earth; before the sea;
before the starry host; before the team of living
creatures swimming in the waters beneath him; before
the animals of every kind, crawling, flying, walking,
running, galloping, slithering, or hopping; before man,
woman, or child; before the trees, plants, and all other
vegetation, he spoke forth himself. We were brought
forth by the word of the living God, through words of
truth in order that we would bring forth life reflecting
all that he is.

If he is first, then he is before every other earthly
relationship. He is before every other cause no matter
how noble. He is before all knowledge and understanding, before science, astrology, and anthropology. He
is before the love of animals, mammals, and all other
life in his world. He is before space and time, before
the study of history, genealogies, and archeology. He is
before me, you and the rest of the world, and the events
that captivate and strive for its attention. He is the
famous one, the First and Last, the Alpha and Omega.
Before the enjoyments we receive from his creation, he
is first. There is no second place for God. It began with
him, by him, and is for him and will end with him,
by him, and for him. Between the beginning and the
end, God will keep speaking, keep reaching, and calling
forth light where there is darkness, so he can come to
have first place even in the darkness of people's lives.

Jesus was our living example of this truth. In Matthew 4, Jesus had just received news that his cousin John had been arrested. He knew John's hour of death was near, so Jesus withdrew from Nazareth and headed into the regions of Galilee. He settled in a place called Capernaum, which was by the sea in the regions of Zebulun and Naphtali.

> The Prophet Isaiah spoke of this hundreds of years beforehand saying, "The land of Zebulun and the land of Naphtali, by the way of the sea, beyond the Jordan, Galilee of the Gentiles. The people who were sitting in darkness saw a great light, and to those who were sitting in the land and shadow of death upon them a light dawned."
>
> —Isaiah 9:1–2

In the land of darkness, the land of Zebulun and Naphtali, the Spirit of God moved with compassion and said, "Let there be light," and the light shone in their darkness, overshadowing their hopelessness to save and restore themselves. So great was its light, the earth quaked beneath its brilliance. The gates of heaven's property were thrown open in the fullness of grace inviting all to enter.

Just as with these ancient cities, so as God has done for the cities of the world. His love was poured out in the very beginning into the darkness itself and continues even this hour. It's the ancient corridor of eternal saving love. God's heart laid bare, stretched across the sky of humanity with fearless transparency and flawless inexpressible hope adorned in holy parchments of flesh.

> In the beginning was the Word, and the Word was with God and the Word was God. He was in the beginning with God. All things came into being by Him, and apart from him nothing came into being that has come into being. In Him was life, and the life was the light of men. And the light shines in the darkness, and the darkness did not comprehend it.
>
> —John 1:1–5

God's love for you is measured by his gift to the world, and he gave all that he had to give. See this gift described for us as penned by the Disciple John, "For God so loved the world that He gave His only begotten Son, that whosoever believeth in him should not perish but have everlasting life" (John 3:16). He gave Jesus; he gave him fully, without hesitancy, without reservation, understanding the loss his heart would know. Grasp this, oh daughter of God, beloved, enveloped in the arms of unconditional love. Cling to this and your heart will know unfailing security that will never disappoint, never abandon and never spare your soul from mercy. It will keep you in the darkest of nights, calm your fear in assailing storms and will carry you all the days of your life. Receive this into the recesses of your being and clothe yourself within its cloak of all sufficiency.

The woman God uses cradles her soul in the depths of this constant—God's love saves, sustains, and keeps. Her life is swallowed up in the ocean of him.

She has been called out of darkness into the manifold presence of his light and her soul is at rest. She has heard the words of the Lord himself calling out to her, "You are the light of the world. A city set on a hill cannot be hidden. Nor do men light a lamp, and put it under the peck-measure, but on the lampstand; and it gives light to all who are in the house. Let your light shine before men in such a way that they may see your good works, and glorify your Father who is in heaven" (Matthew 5:14–16). And in the hearing, she answers; she unashamedly responds by rising up the city of her life that all may see. And when darkness falls, her life gives light to many who have lost their way.

Hear this, receive it in full faith; God has looked upon your darkness, upon your life and calling out to you declares, "Let there be light in her, let there be God in her." You are the light of his world. The light house of his favor and presence. He calls even now to you, to the deepest part for light to come forth. Will you answer his voice? Will you break forth from the shadows of the earth releasing the darkness from your life, bringing forth the light of God? This is good in his sight, for she recalls the Creator's words, "And God saw the light and it was good." Some of you have stayed in the shadows far too long in fear of coming into the light because of what it might expose. We must not let the fear of truth restrain our yielding to the calling we know is of God. In this light is mercy, strength, and every good thing we need to live as he intended for us to live.

Let him shine through you, from you, and in you, permeating the world around you. Those in darkness will see it and will give him glory. This is God's will for every life that has answered the call of his creative power. We must be separate; our life must release every yoke of bondage and every tie to the world still in darkness. A woman God uses must have no intimacy with the darkness, no shred of acceptance of its presence in her midst, and absolutely no ties demanding her allegiance and loyalty. Her life is not her own, knowing that it is God who has said, "Light shall shine out of darkness," and is the one who has shone in her heart to give the light of the knowledge of the glory of God in the face of Christ (2 Corinthians 4:6). Her purpose is to shine, to set the spotlight of her life upon the face of Christ. He has her heart, her love, and her life.

Each day is filled with the promise of revealing him to a lost and dying world. She anticipates the morning in full assurance, knowing that it is him who lives in and through her. She fears nothing, no one, and no condition of life she may come to experience or find herself in; it's only a stage upon which she can declare his praise—a platform to shine a light upon the one who is light. Her countenance speaks her heart. She cannot hide the light captured within. This radiant woman is living truth before the world, choosing whether in deed or word to honor the pledge of her allegiance, "I have been crucified with Christ; and it is no longer I who live, but Christ lives in me; and the life which I now live in the flesh I live by faith in the Son of God, who loved me, and delivered Himself up for me" (Galatians 2:20). This woman knows she must die before Christ can live. She releases everything dear, all that she has control over, and even more difficult, those things she does not. Her dreams, her plans, her way, her strength and power are laid down. Her identity is gone, so she can assume the one of Christ who lives in her knowing that death is swallowed up in victory! She is steadfast, immovable, always abounding in the work of the Lord, knowing that her labors for him are never in vain (1 Corinthians 15:54,58). In godly sincerity, she offers up thanks to God, who always leads her in triumph in Christ and manifests through her the sweet aroma of the knowledge of him in every place. She is a fragrance of Jesus among those who are being saved and even among those who are perishing—those who are in the darkness. And like the light placed in the darkness, so she is in the midst of the perishing (2 Corinthians 2:14–15).

His aroma, when poured out, is sweet, sacrificial, and purposefully beautiful when offered freely. Bringing us to this place of emptying is altogether unlovely at times. Let me share with you a story about a man named Saul, who heard the voice of God as he shown his light into the darkness. This man was no ordinary man. Born of privilege and honor, there was no expense spared for his education. He had the world's greatest teacher as his mentor, and he excelled in every academic and spiritual area known. He was upstanding and held a position of authority among the religious leaders. He was more zealous than most and passionate in his faith, not counting the cost. He was a self appointed avenger for God with whom he gave his full attention to carry out. After all, it was his duty to save the name of God and protect his holy position in the lives of his people. Upon his self appointed mission, Saul journeyed to Damascus to arrest and even destroy those he deemed as enemies of God. Upon the road, the scriptures describe what happens:

> And it came about as he journeyed, he was approaching Damascus, and suddenly a light from heaven flashed around him; and he fell to the ground, and heard a voice saying to him, "Saul, Saul, why are you persecuting me?" And he said, "Who art thou, Lord?" And he said, "I am Jesus whom you are persecuting. but rise, and enter the city and it shall be told you what you must do." And the men who traveled with him stood speechless, hearing the voice, but seeing no one. And Saul got up from the ground, and though his eyes were open, he could see nothing."
>
> —Acts 9:3–8

This was the death of and the dying of Saul and the living of Christ within him. His life, although full of good and zealous deeds, had never encountered the light from heaven. Christ said, "I am the Light of the world; he who follows Me shall not walk in the darkness, but shall have the light of life" (John 8:12). Sometimes he has to cut us off from seeing in order to open our eyes to him. When God veils one area, it's only so he can shine a spotlight on another of which we would never have seen any other way. "In hope we have been saved, but hope that is seen is not hope; for why does one also hope for what he sees? But if we hope for what we do not see, with perseverance we wait eagerly for it" (Romans 8:25–26). This is what happened in the life of Saul. If you are familiar with the New Testament, you will know this man by the name of Paul, the bondservant of Jesus Christ. Upon the Damascus Road, God looked down upon the darkness of Saul's life and said, "Let there be light." And a light from heaven flashed around him, and he fell on the ground, and for the first time, he encountered Jesus. Light penetrated the darkness and the earth trembled. Beloved one, it quaked beneath the footsteps of the life of Paul because great was his light.

Jesus wants to do the same for every woman and man who will do just as the Apostle Paul did—fall to the ground before him, speak his name upon your lips and call him Lord. And just as Paul did that day upon the dusty road to Damascus, rise up and walk from that day forward in the light, hoping in what is not seen with all perseverance. "Faith comes by hearing and hearing by the word of God" (Romans 10:17), not from the seeing. Until we let go of the need to see, touch, feel, and understand, we will shackle the work of God in our own lives. Just like the need that Thomas had, to touch the wounds of Jesus before he would believe he was alive. Little did he know that the Light of the World had come forth from the tomb of darkness.

We read in John 20:1 that "while it was still dark, Mary Magdalene came early to the tomb." Darkness had fallen, draping itself over the land in the middle of the day as the Light of the World was dying upon the cross that he might live in us. Mary was desperately looking for the Light that she had come to know and love. But great was the hopelessness beneath the shadows of the night as she made her way to the tomb. Three days she had been searching, longing to feel and know his presence. And as if God could wait no longer, not wanting the sun to steal Jesus's thunder, he commanded it to keep its place, for the sun was not needed on this morning for the greater light was about to break forth. In utter darkness, the Spirit of God was moving over the surface of the deep waiting to call forth life, he rises to give the call. He stands in full power armed with untold wisdom and shrouded in the purest glory; the army of angels make themselves ready just as they had done in the beginning of time. They are ready to shout, sing, attend, take flight, and lift up a war cry to the Ancient of Days. His eyes a flame, his hair as white as the starry hosts and enthroning his glow is a rainbow of every color known to man. As the eyes of Sovereignty looked down over the darkness of death while it was still dark, he spoke, "Let there be light!" And the earth trembled, the stone rolled away from its crevasse, and like the Shekinah glory stationed upon the holy mount, Light ascended up from the pit of sheol, crying, "Let there be light!" And the darkness fled. And God saw that it was good.

You are the light of the world, a city set high for all to see. You are the light of the world, a city to display the glory of God. You are the light of the world, a city that has risen above all that is earthbound. He spoke over you and cried, "Let there be light." Are you light? Are you living beautifully out loud for his glory? Does your face show Jesus? Are your eyes aflame with the love of Jesus? Let there be light, precious one, let there be light.

Step up to this truth without apology—live out loud, shine bright, radiate Jesus without fear. Refuse to live an ordinary life, cease the day at hand, knowing that "Darkness is passing away and the true light is already shining" (1 John 2:8). Refuse to settle, refuse compromise, refuse meritocracy, and refuse to cover the light within you. Be a beacon of hope, a light to show the way for all who are hopelessly lost. Set this in your heart to do, and God will use you to bring it about. And the earth will tremble beneath your footsteps.

Write out your thoughts, your confessions before the Lord:

_____

_____

_____

_____

_____

_____

"Do not speak unless you can improve the silence"

A Life-Giving Woman

"Set a guard, O Lord, over my mouth; keep watch over the door of my lips"

—Psalm 141:3

As a young child, I learned the familiar rhyme as so many children do, "Sticks and stones may break my bones, but words will never hurt me." No matter how loudly I sang this, my heart knew there was no truth in what it said. Words did hurt and sometimes the wounds they inflict last a lifetime. I dreaded going to the bus stop in the mornings and especially if I had to wait any length of time because it meant there was more opportunity for the other children to make fun of me. I was skinny, timid, shy, and my face had the kisses of the sun upon it—lovingly referred to as "freckles." My hair was an auburn color with highlights from the sun coursing through it, and it was usually, much like me, quite a mess. I seldom brushed it when my mother wasn't around. I was very much into the all natural look! I was small for my age and so I was picked on a good bit. But the worst was being teased for the way I looked.

I can still remember one particular time when the teasing made a lasting impression upon me as a young girl. My school had chosen two girls to win the Junior Deputy Camp award, and I was one of the girls chosen. To this day, I still don't know why I won it. I wasn't even a Junior Deputy! But at the time I didn't care, I just knew I was going to camp that summer and that's something I had never done before. My sweet little papa came and took me to meet the bus the day we headed to camp. I can still see him standing in the courthouse parking lot in the heat of summer refusing to leave until the bus got out of sight. I loved my papa so much and most of all I knew that he loved me. Waves of homesick washed over me as he disappeared from my view and all of a sudden camp wasn't as exciting as it had been up to that moment. I wanted to stand up and yell, "Stop the bus, I want to get off." But the courage to do that would never come.

We made our way until finally arriving at the camp, where I would spend the next week just trying to survive homesickness. It was an old military base which had a lot of old equipment to play on and statues to take interesting pictures by. Being new to this camp stuff, I quickly attached myself to the other girl from my school that was also chosen to go. Her name was Jenny and she was tall, beautiful, and extremely confident—something I definitely was not. She was also bossy, but I didn't mind it so much as long as she would let me stick with her like glue! Jenny would leave a lasting impression upon me that I would battle for years to come.

The week moved by as slow as any week could and every night I cried myself to sleep because I was so homesick. I had never been away from home before except to my papa's and this was certainly not my papa and granny's house. The last night of camp finally arrived, and to celebrate the whole camp was going to have a beauty contest. Yes, you heard me right, a beauty contest! What were they thinking? Anyway, each barrack had to choose one girl to represent their group in the contest. As our bunker of girls gathered together to talk about it, Jenny chimed in with these words, "Let's put her in the contest as a joke." I looked and to my surprise, she was pointing at me. The other girls laughed and it was unanimous—I would be the joke of the beauty contest.

I remember running away as fast as my little legs could carry me until I was sure I was far enough away for no one to hear or see me, and I began to sob. I never felt like I was pretty, although like every other little girl, I wanted to be. But no one had ever confirmed for me out loud that I wasn't pretty. But this seemed to confirm my worst nightmare: I wasn't only not pretty, but I was actually ugly. I was but a joke to the other girls. It's heartbreaking for anyone to hear words that belittle or make fun of them, but it's crushing for young girls. The effect of that moment would continue to mold and shape my thinking for many years, even into my parenting years. It's a time in my life's history line that is marked with pain and great impression. It would be years before I would find deliverance from the shackles those words anchored upon my heart. You see, "Death and life are in the power of the tongue" (Proverbs 8:21).

We all have those monuments that have been erected in our lives, built upon the foundation of another's words. They come quickly but remain a lifetime. I've heard the heartbreak of countless women who have suffered fatal wounds emotionally because of something that was said to them once or over the course of a lifetime. Some words cut deeper than others but nevertheless leave us wounded and often crippled from living. The experiences will continue to cultivate the fruit of insecurity, low self-esteem, fear, intimidation, and a need to be accepted, a need for approval no matter the cost. It will stifle and even ruin other relationships because we fear rejection again, because very hurtful words to us are received as a form of rejection. We can build up another for years, and in one careless, thoughtless, selfish moment utter one untamed thought and leave it all in ruins.

Words are very powerful—more powerful, more influential than we could ever imagine. Once spoken, unlike written words, they can never be erased from the pages of our mind. They can never be fully eradicated from our memories. They are eternal forces impacting the lives they find lodging in. This is why we are instructed in the book of James 1:19 to be "quick to hear, slow to speak." The slowness gives us time to ponder our words before releasing them out into the atmosphere of a person's life. Slowness speaks of weighing it out against eternity and the situation at hand, sifting it through the holiness of God to see if it passes through, allowing us to give our words freedom, knowing they have been approved by God. Understanding the power of spoken words is the first step to setting up a guard about your mouth and a must for the woman who longs to be used by God. Listen to the words of James once more:

> For we all stumble in many ways. If anyone does
> not stumble in what he says, he is a perfect man,

able to bridle the whole body as well. Now, if we put the bits into the horses' mouths so that they may obey us, we direct their entire body as well. Behold, the ships also, tough they are so great and are driven by strong winds, are still directed by a very small rudder, wherever the inclination of the pilot desires. So also the tongue is a small part of the body and yet it boasts of great things.

—James 1:1–5

Did you see it? The tongue, although a small part of the body, has the power to turn even the greater forces in the direction it wants them to go. James compares the tongue to the rudder of a ship and the bridle of a horse, both which direct and harness great power although very small in comparison. It's true, the pen is mightier than the sword because it is used to pen words. The sword can wound, threaten, direct, take hostage, and even kill, yet the pen is deemed mightier, why? Because words can wound, threaten, direct, take hostage, and even kill—over and over again. A sword gives one fatal strike and its over, but the tongue will continue its destruction long after the first wound has been inflicted. It deposits a long lasting poison in the soul that will course through the veins of one's life long after the initial wounding has seemingly healed. Words have power. If we read further in James, we see the effects of the tongue long after the words are spoken.

And the tongue is a fire, the very world of iniquity; the tongue is set among our members as that which defiles the entire body, and sets on fire the course of our life, and is set on fire by hell. For every species of beasts and birds, of reptiles and creatures of the sea, is tamed, and has been tamed by the human race. But no one can tame the tongue; it is a restless evil and full of deadly poison. With it, we bless our Lord and Father; and with it we curse men, who have been made in the likeness of God; from the same mouth come both blessing and cursing. My brethren, these things ought not to be this way.

—James 1:6–10

The tongue sets on fire the very course of one's life, yours and mine and those we have influence over with our words. Sometimes the utterances of one may start a very small fire, but another's words may be the fuel that accelerates it. Fire needs a source of fuel, listen to the wise counsel:

For lack of wood the fire goes out and where there is no whisperer, contention quiets down. Like charcoal to hot embers and wood to fire, so is a contentious man to kindle strife. The words of a whisperer are like dainty morsels and they go down into the innermost parts of a body.

—Proverbs 26:20–22

It has been said, "Unless you can improve the silence, then don't speak." Words to live by! How we need to be quick to hear but slow, very slow to speak, oh daughter. Great has been the fall of many simply because they had those in their lives who were faithful to fuel the flame sparked by another in dishonor.

Have you ever been a participator in the fire? Have you been the victim? Have you ever taken the time to look back at the smoke, rising from the ruins of another's life and known remorse? Have you been the one who struck the match to another's life? Sometimes we know the power of our words and choose to speak them anyway because we have an agenda of our own we want to accomplish. Maybe it's to belittle another in order to exalt ourselves or to destroy another's reputation to feed our own insecurities and jealousy. Behind every word spoken is either motive or ignorance. I don't know which is more dangerous, those who know the power of words and choose not to tame them or those who have yet to learn their power and speak them impulsively.

Ashamed to confess, I've been in my lifetime. I've used words so carelessly not recognizing or refusing to recognize their power, and I've also used them to bring about my own agenda to manipulate the future events. These are things I am most ashamed of but one that I have come to recognize early on in my walk with the Lord, as he extended a magnitude of patience and mercies to me in the correction process. I love him all the more for it! I have certainly not attained absolute control of my tongue, in fact far from it, but one thing I do, I press on to that end. I determine to speak slowly and be conscious to hear—to be seen and not so much heard. I resolve to think about this over, "Unless I can improve the silence, don't speak." These words have made me their captive and for the better.

God has taught me from the passages of James (chapter 1) that the secret of self control and the bringing about of holiness is the determination to control my tongue by making it God's prisoner. If we can tame the tongue, the Scripture teaches, we are also able to control our whole body as well. This is a secret of spiritual giants and we will do well to get it. It's not so much about controlling our bodies as much as it is about controlling our tongues. Because from our tongue comes life or death, not only to others within ear shot, but to us as well. Narrow your discipline to training your speech and the rest will fall gently with great purpose into its ordained places. Show me a woman who has her mouth under control, and I'll show you a woman God can use. Show me a woman whose mouth speaks at will whether openly or privately, and I'll show you a woman God cannot use.

Proverbs 9:11 declares, "The mouth of the righteous is a fountain of life." The woman God uses will commit her mouth to righteousness giving forth life when she speaks. She knows "where there are many words, transgression is unavoidable, but he who restrains his lips is wise. The tongue of the righteous is as choice silver…and the lips of the righteous feed many" (Proverbs 10:19–21). The woman God uses is intentional in her speech, guarded with her tongue, realizing the accountability that comes with such a powerful weapon. Just as her words are powerful to destroy, they are just as powerful to build up. Just as they have the ability to bring death, they have the ability to impart life. The most obvious sign of a woman God uses is her speech. Our lips will give our hearts away revealing who it belongs to. She stands apart from every other woman because she is prudent, God fearing and reverently purposeful in every word she forms upon her tongue. She speaks a rare and beautiful language—the language of grace.

With every audience God gives us, whether one or many, we have the blessed privilege of pouring out the living waters of the Lord. She will ponder how to respond and what to say because she has set her heart on righteousness (Proverbs 15:28). She knows that "the heart of the wise teaches his mouth, and adds persuasiveness to his lips because pleasant words are a honeycomb, sweet to the soul and healing to the bones" (Proverbs 16:23–24). Maybe you have experienced this yourself when you've been in the presence of such a woman. You walk away refreshed, encouraged, and wanting to be more of the woman God wants you to be because you have been in her presence. Righteous words nourish us, they give life to the dead areas within us, and they awaken the sleeping places to rise and be more for God. It's like being in a spiritual hospital, receiving the medicine your soul has languished for. The atmosphere around her is different—it's filled with hope, joy, and peace. Her speech is seasoned with grace, falling upon those who have lost meaning in living.

D.L. Moody has seven principles that he lived by in order to be used by God to the fullest. One of those principles was this, "Never speak or repeat anything about another person that will bring them harm." This was among his seven, right up there with praying, studying the Bible and witnessing. This shows the wisdom Mr. Moody had in the holy bridle he had fastened upon his mouth. His mouth belonged to the Lord, not to him, and most of all not to the world. He refused to ever repeat anything about anyone, even if it was true, that would shed a bad light upon them or bring them some sort of pain or shame. He refused to allow himself to be the giver of death in another's life on any level but especially through his words. He lived by, "He who covers a transgression seeks love, but he who repeats a matter separates intimate friends" (Proverbs 17:19). He sought love in every word he spoke, and God used this man to bring countless souls to glory. "Now abide faith, hope, love, these three; but the greatest of these is love" (1 Corinthians 13:13).

Sometimes the way we can love the most is by choosing not to belittle or destroy another's testimony by something we've heard or know to be true. The woman who guards her mouth preserves life (Proverbs 13:3). She loves unconditionally. Listen to how God describes love for us:

> Love is patient, love is kind, and is not jealous; love does not brag and is not arrogant, does not act unbecomingly; it does not seek its own, is not provoked, does not take into account a wrong suffered, does not rejoice in unrighteousness, but rejoices with the truth; bears all things, believes all things, hopes all things, endures all things. Love never fails.
>
> —1 Corinthians 13:4–8

Our speech is affected by each and every one of these duties of love. It is the duty of love to exercise patience when it speaks and like the Proverbs 31 woman, "the speaking of kindness is upon her tongue" (verse 26). She does not allow jealousy to destroy another by what she says because she will not brag nor will she act unbecomingly. She never uses her opportunities to seek her own welfare because she seeks the good of those around her. She will not allow her heart to be provoked to anger and pour out words in retribution. This woman will never remember how another has hurt her when she is speaking about them. She will not use these opportunities to get even or strike back, because that would be unrighteous and this brings her grief. Her heart rejoices to speak of God's truth because his love never fails.

Words can bring healing to the wounded places, or they can open up the wound, bringing a fresh wave of grief and pain all over again. It's the slander of others that keep wounds from healing. I know the pain that words can cause. I've been a victim to them as many of you have been as well. You can live a good life in the Lord, serve faithfully for thirty years and no one will really remember that about you. But if you blow it one time, act unbecoming one time, or if someone else speaks ill of you or slanders you, all the thirty years of good are forgotten. All people will remember is the bad. Why? Power and life are in the tongue. The sad thing is that there are always the repeat offenders, the bad will keep showing up, retold with the new added for flavor, and your testimony dies a slow and painful death. There is power and life in the tongue—in our words. How the world languishes for life-giving waters that the language of grace pours forth.

We can destroy the work of God with one ill-spoken thing whether it's true or someone's version of the truth. The greatest grievance to the name of God in this is the fact that it happens in the body of Christ. I've seen the posse in church form and go on a man hunt with their words. They want to take the preacher down or another leader or member because they were hurt by them or disappointed. They start the strife, build their team, and spread the word to anyone and everyone who will listen. People will believe a lie before they will believe the truth often times. Before you know it, a good testimony is destroyed because someone refused to set a guard about their mouth. Slander sets a church on fire with destruction and burns down the lives of God's people in the process. I've seen the ruins that the words of others have left behind. Those ruins have been my own life at times. Words are so powerful, daughter, they are so destructive yet can be altogether lovely when purposed to be so.

But God has given us a healing balm to apply in the hearts of the hurting, beloved. Listen to his words to us, "A soothing tongue is a tree of life" (Proverbs 15:23) and "Anxiety in the heart of a man weighs it down, but a good word makes it glad" (Proverbs 12:25). There are those who have never heard a gentle and kind word spoken to them. Everyone longs to hear kindness, to be spoken too in love and fullness of acceptance. They long for a harbor of safety in the presence of another because they trust in them to only do good even when they are parted. Some have never heard the words "I love you," "You are beautiful," "I am here for you," "I'm so sorry," "What a great job you did," or "I care about you." They long to hear words of life because they've only known death, sorrow, and pain.

I've watched the faces of my own girls light up with such life and joy when I've clapped for them, cheered them on, and showered them with my words of "you are the bomb!" Like every other child, they desperately wanted validation. They were like thirsty sponges soaking up every word spoken to them, and I loved to speak truth and strength into them, building them up to be strong and beautiful women. It was like planting a garden of joy in their little lives, and I had the blessed privilege of watching it grow and mature and then see them plant their own gardens of joy in their adult lives. We know that children are very impressionable, but we never lose the ability to be affected, to be impressionable. No matter our age, our status, or maturity we will always have a certain amount of pliability that gives to outward influences. Never underestimate the impression words can leave upon your life. They are like bank deposits into our beings that gain strength with time.

You may be one of those women, and if you are, you are not alone. Let this be the driving force in your life to be a life giving woman with your words—a woman who speaks the language of grace. Pour out hope and healing into the lives of others and you will wash away your own pain in the process. It's the power of words. Not only are you speaking words of life but you will be hearing them as they are released out into the life of another, and you see the beauty of God captivate, restore, rescue, encourage, strengthen and fill with unspeakable joy. The aroma you leave will linger long after you have left. Choose to be a beautiful woman in words, not merely the outward adornment. Be purposeful to build up, not tear down, defend not destroy, love not hate, and watch God use you more and more. And for every hurtful word you may have spoken, go before the Lord and confess it and then go to the one you offended and apply the healing balm of life with your words of apology. Seek their forgiveness.

God longs to use us, but we must long to be used. He waits for us to surrender everything to him including our ability to speak. Jesus told his disciples that we will give an account of every careless word spoken (Matthew 12:36). That's a monument of accountability when we stop and view all the words we have spoken over the course of our lives. It is a very sobering thought to say the least. How many times have we spoken a word in haste, without thought to its repercussions and passed on our way never realizing the affects that would follow? Are your words careless, without forethought or purpose? Sometimes we hurt others by our words without intending to because we did not stop to access the damage ahead of time. Careless words hold just as much accountability as purposeful ones. There is no difference in the presence of God.

We don't need huge platforms to impact lives, only a consecrated tongue unto God. Our words will outlive us when we are gone so make them count. Plant hope, love, faith, courage, strength, and joy in others. Speak your faith into the next generation with boldness and powerful purpose leaving a holy legacy after you are gone. Invest in lives through the power of your words, making spiritual deposits into them. Speak with purity always building up and bringing honor to God. Magnify Jesus with your words and draw people to him with speech that has been seasoned with prayer and devotion to his word. Determine to allow no unwholesome word to proceed from your mouth except that which is good for edification, and God will use you in innumerable lives across his globe.

I hear women all the time say, "I wish God would use me." Or they have fallen prey to the belief that God can't or never will use them because they have nothing to offer. This is but a lie produced by the enemy of old down through the ages of time to keep God's people from serving him. Everyone of us have been given the power of words, whether in spoken, written, signed, or in song. We have this most powerful responsible gift. We can all be used with just this one amazing instrument. We don't need money or talent, not even fame or position, only a heart that is willing. He leaves the choice to us but gives this gift freely no matter what we decide to do. This is the platform God gives to each of us. We all have it, and we all have the same potential to do great things with it. It's the influence of words; the might of and driving power to declare, destroy, build up, deliver, protect and save, find and lose.

Set your life ablaze for his kingdom and guard your mouth as memorial for the Lord. Use the power he has given you to bring healing to those who have been wounded so deeply. Apply God's holy salve of promise to the hopeless, and give the gift of joy with your mouth in conversation. Protect others by denying yourself and singing their praise for edification. Tell someone they can't and they never will, but share courage and they will be unstoppable. Determine to not be a hindrance but rather a force of freedom for the faint in heart. Lay every word upon the altar of surrender, and God will send down the fire upon your life. Allow your mouth to be the song of heaven upon the earth and watch your life multiply his name in all the earth.

I pray with my whole being that you will recognize the powerful gift given to you and the accountability that is attached to its wonder. Become, strive, reach, even yearn to be that woman who speaks kindness always, loves with every word, and gives life to everyone she encounters along the way. To do so, oh daughter, is to set the world ablaze with the beauty of God, burning away all that is barren in order to bring forth new life. Will you be that woman?

Take a moment to write down your promise and thoughts to God concerning your speech.

_____

_____

_____

_____

_____

_____

_____

_____

_____

A Voice in the Wilderness

"And the Lord was adding to their number day by day those who were being saved."

—Acts 2:47

I remember, as a young girl, my mother and I along with the pastor's wife, walking door to door to witness and invite people to church. Although, I didn't understand what was going on, I only knew that I usually got a long stick of bubble gum to keep me occupied for the duration of the evening. Little did I know these women were warring for souls, speaking the name of Jesus to all who would listen to their words of salvation. I also remember many doors being slammed in their faces, many rejections and words of insult as they walked away from the house. Not everyone welcomes the name of Jesus and the salvation which he alone can give. God taught me early on not to expect acceptance when speaking for him. Many years have passed since then and today is no different; people still reject, despise, and refuse the only name given under heaven whereby men must be saved (Acts 4:12). Yet the faithfulness of God who wishes for none to perish but for all to come to repentance and a saving knowledge of Jesus Christ (2 Peter 3:9) calls even now to every lost soul upon the earth. His voice has never faltered throughout the ages, never ceased to cry out to all who have lost their way.

The wall of hatred erected between salvation and condemnation still stands between life and death. It's a barrier between light and darkness. This wall is fortified, high and impenetrable apart from the power of God. But the sound rising from their peaks resonates with such desperation; from one side it's the cry of agony and pain ascending from the despair beneath. It's the resonance of the lost—never satisfied, never with hope. Such despair is heard even up to the gateway of heaven to make its plea before the Holy One. Faithful is he to answer, even though they know not that he is the answer! They march on into eternal separation from God day by day, hour by hour. I heard an old preacher, with such passion and brokenness as I have ever seen say, "Can you hear it child of God, do you hear that sound, that unforgettable sound? The sound that robs you, like a thief in the night, of your slumbering rest... it's footsteps that I hear...the sound is so loud, one can hardly drown out its noise. It's an army marching in perfect unison, marching into an eternal hell." His words still pierce my soul to this day.

I too was among the throngs in utter abandonment to the penalties of my sin. I was among the dead even though my heart still beat within its chambers. My life was in bondage, and I did not know how to free myself. I struggled to be good, but the good I tried so passionately to accomplish passed me by, never willing to make its lodging place in my life. No one had to tell me I needed God, I just didn't know how to get to him. I knew of him, even believed in him but it ended there; it never went any further. I was seventeen years old and full of misery, disappointment and mounds of guilt covered my heart and mind. I wanted peace. I tried so hard to escape from the memories of the guilt I had gained because of my many sins. God seemed so far away and rightly so in my eyes. After all, why would he want to save me? How could he forgive me of all of my sins? My sins were greater than God's forgiveness in my eyes. Finally, when I could bear the shame no longer, I cried from the deepest part of my being, and I kept crying out until my cry ascended above the wall of my condemnation and reached the throne of my God. He heard me—but greater still, I heard him! God had not only opened his ears to hear my plea to be saved, but he answered in full faithfulness and without hesitation. His name was Reverend Buddy Norton. I want his name upon the pages of this book because he has been faithful to pursue souls like no one else I've ever known. His name deserves to grace the pages of this book, especially for this writer because it is to him I owe an eternal debt of gratitude for pursuing my soul for Jesus. Thank you for answering the cry of such a young sinful woman, who was hopelessly lost and on her way to hell. Only heaven will reveal the crowns you have earned for your King.

Brother Buddy took the time, made the time, and was urgent to give his time to win the lost at any cost. He was attentive to the cry of the lost. This was his spiritual secret, hear it once again precious one—he was attentive to the cry of the lost. Have I been so busy that I've drowned out the noise of the lost who are marching into the gates of hell every day? Is my heart so in tune with self that I have become calloused to the needs of eternity? Am I willing to lift my voice and say, "This way, come this way and know the salvation of Jesus?" How many tears have I shed for the countless souls who are dying without Jesus? Does my heart break over the condemned? Do I even care about the lost? As long as my own family is saved, I'm happy and that's really all that matters, right? Isn't it the responsibility of the preacher and evangelist to win them? Will God hold me accountable for all the lost who have crossed my path, and I failed to share Jesus with them? Can God use me to win the lost? Difficult questions, I know, but they are questions that need to be answered in light of eternity. I pray you won't put this book down but hear what God's word says to each of us no matter what our callings may be.

Some of the most fearful times of my life have been when the Lord has prompted me to witness and share my faith. I began early on in my walk with God in striving to witness because out of the goodness of God, I had a pastor who modeled that for me. He lived this every day of his life, and if you ever had a conversation with him, especially for the first time, he was going to cover with you the condition of your soul. It was just a given with him and something he was known for. For the lost it was the question of, "Is your soul saved?" For the saved, it was, "Is your soul right with God?" So I came to the point in my early Christian years to become a woman of passionate witnessing. I began with all I knew to do and that was with Christian tracks that explained what I felt I couldn't. My first attempt was at a gas pump; there was a woman pumping gas next to me. After pumping far more gas than I had intended, trying to work up the courage, I finally just stuck it on her windshield when she went in to pay and drove away like a bullet! I felt as though I had just bombarded hell with a water pistol! God was and still is so very patient with me. I was relieved and proud all at the same time; neither of which God was probably proud of.

Though my start to witnessing was rough at first going, I kept with it even though there were times I thought I was just going to throw up because of my nerves. I share this with you because I want you to know that even Bible teachers and preachers have to start somewhere, and it's usually in fear and trembling and with many blunders. But God is faithful to grow you and bless your faithfulness. The greater the sacrifice, the greater the fire. I continued with tracks and volunteered to help with altar call for the services. And every time, every time…did I say every time, I had to totally rely on God for what to say. This is why most of us will never try and witness because we don't want to be put into a position where we have to trust God in the moment. It's easy to say you trust God, but to actually have to trust him when you are face to face with someone not knowing what to do is totally a different matter. Trust isn't present until every other support is absent. God will use us if we are willing to trust him and be obedient to share Jesus. Remember Jesus's words, "If you deny me before men, then I'll deny you before the Father." I believe that this holds true for witnessing. If we share Jesus before people, then Jesus will intercede on our behalf before God to help us and support us in the work. Hear the words of Isaiah:

> For as the rain and the snow come down from heaven, and do not return there without watering the earth, and making it bear and sprout, and furnishing seed to the sower and bread to the eater; so shall My word which goes forth from My mouth; it shall not return to me empty, without accomplishing what I desire, and without succeeding in the matter for which I sent it. For you will go out with joy, and be led forth with peace; The mountains and the hills will break forth into shouts of joy before you.
>
> Isaiah 55:10–12

When we speak his word, when we speak of Jesus, who is the Word, he will accomplish the work he desires. He says of the vessels through which his words are spoken that we will have joy, peace, and strength, when the price seems too high to pay. I've been in numerous situations where witnessing was made easy, where it seemed as if the mountains broke forth before me with shouts of joy and then I've had other times where seemed the mountains were raised before me. I can only say to this that the enemy is ever present ready to snatch the precious seed from the sower. But God is faithful even on the other side of the mountain.

I can't say there is any one proven method for sharing the love of God by explaining the truth of Jesus. But I do know that Jesus shared with those who gave him their attention. He did not throw the pearl of truth out into the air haphazardly. But when the eyes were fixed upon him, he spoke with purpose, intentionally giving the truth of the Father. With every encounter God gives us, whether it is in a coffee shop, a restaurant, the mall, dentist or doctor's office, in a grocery store or beauty parlor, we are to make the most of the time. "But sanctify Christ as Lord in your hearts always being ready to make a defense to everyone who asks you to give an account for the hope that is in you, yet with gentleness and reverence" (1 Peter 3:15). Once Christ has been sanctified in our hearts, our readiness to share him must take front and center stage. Every encounter is a platform from God upon which we can share his salvation. Learn to see these encounters as divine, appointed by heaven, and embrace them without shame and without fear.

The woman God uses will be a woman who is always ready, always looking for these platforms to speak of Jesus. She searches, prays with great expectancy the day as it rises, wondering who will be snatched from the jaws of death today. Her heart is for the lost because she knows it's first and foremost upon the Father's heart, and she lives to please him. There is no fear because she knows it is he who will do the work through her, and those who reject her words are really rejecting his. Her heart trusts completely in him, knowing he will give her the words to speak and direct her paths to the one who needs to hear it. Jesus was not ashamed to hang on the cross before the world for her, so she is not ashamed to share his cross with the world. She knows her time upon the earth is but a vapor, therefore she pours herself out into every soul that crosses her path.

Her delight is in the Lord and to magnify him in all the earth. She will not rest until everyone has heard and until then she presses on, refusing to look back upon past failures only ahead to the new day before her.

The longing to be this woman has continued to grow within my heart and is still increasing today. My heart stirs when I think of sharing Jesus with someone or speaking of his goodness and mercies to one who has never heard or needs to hear it once again. Your heart will never know a greater joy than knowing you've been used by him in the life of another. I can attest that he will completely remove your fear and all anxiety you have in witnessing and sharing the love of Jesus if you will step out in obedience. He meets us at our place of obedience, never before it. It takes great courage to lay hold of the calling to witness and believe God for the help to carry it out and the help to bring about good from it. He will never mislead you, and his timing is impeccable. I can attest to this time and time again as I have witnessed this in my own life as I have said yes to his tender promptings.

One such time that I love to share is when I was in an IHOP restaurant in Lagrange, Georgia. I was speaking at a Women's Conference there, and in the hotel I was staying in, there was adjoined to it an IHOP. Now you must first know two things; I love blueberry pancakes, and I don't get them very often. This particular evening, I was tired from speaking all day, and I hadn't eaten as it is typical for me on such occasions. We had just had a wonderful time in the Lord and souls were saved, of which even now I praise him for! I wanted to go and have some blueberry pancakes and coffee for a late dinner. I was so excited about the thought of it, I could hardly wait; besides, I knew IHOP was open 24 hours! I asked my assistant Debbie if she would go with me since the other women on our team had already eaten. She gladly accepted my dinner invitation! We were seated, and I didn't even take time to look at the menu. I knew exactly what I wanted—blueberry pancakes and coffee. Just the thought of it made my mouth water.

After placing my order, the Lord drew my attention to rest upon a woman across the restaurant sitting all alone in a booth. There was no food on the table and in front of her was a mound of papers that looked like letters of some sort. Her face was conspicuously distraught. She kept running both hands through her hair and then coming to rest her face in them as if in utter despair. Her head kept looking down over the copious pile of papers set before her. She had such a look of despair upon her face, and I could see her lips mumble something over and over again. Immediately, I looked away saying to the Lord, "I don't have time for this, I have my blueberry pancakes on the way!" I know that all too familiar prompting of his, when he wants me to speak to someone. He kept speaking to my heart these words, "Go tell her that I know about her and that I do care." I struggled, even explaining to the Lord that this woman was going to think that I was nuts. Couldn't I just go and witness to her plain out?—but after I had eaten my blueberry pancakes of course!

I battled for the longest time there in that booth even telling the Lord, "You can send Debbie, she's already eaten!" I know what you're thinking, "She just threw her under the bus" and you are right—anything for blueberry pancakes. But God wasn't having it! He was clearly sending me with a specific message to share from him. I excused myself from the table and headed over to hers. As I approached, I told the Father, "Now, I'm saying this because you have told me too, so please know what you're talking about!" Of course that was my flesh that really wasn't interested in the Lord's work at the moment. I introduced myself and told the woman these words, "I know that you don't know me and what I'm going to say to you is going to sound crazy, but God wanted me to come over here and tell you that he does know about you and he does care." I felt a great sense of relief to have it out there and thought that now I would be free to go back to my table. Again, God wasn't having it.

The lady looked at me in such shock. Once what I said began to sink in, she began to well up with tears. As the tears began rolling down her face, she told me how she had just been asking the Lord, "Do you know about me and do you even care?" Needless to say, my heart just broke with the thought of the struggle I had put up with the Lord in being his vessel. For the next hour and a half, this precious woman began to pour out her story to me and the catastrophic events that had assailed her. She was older, single, and had no children, no one to turn to. All she had was her job and that too was at the risk of being lost. She didn't know where to turn and so in her desperation, she called out to God there in the IHOP restaurant. God does know what he's doing and his heart is to reach the heart of his child even if he has to do it in an IHOP. Although she was a Christian, she still needed the love of Jesus poured out upon her at that moment. God brought her hope and reassured her of his faithfulness and his awareness of her life.

Sometimes God will send us to speak words of salvation for the lost, and sometimes he will send us to share words of hope for the saved. Either way, we must keep our hearts pliable to walk in obedience when he summons. Our mind must be alert to those around us searching for the one God has his eye on to reach with his love and faithful mercies. But for all the times we tell him no, what happens to the one who so desperately needs to find the Lord? We don't need the platforms built by man or to have a title behind our name to be his voice, only a willing heart. Jesus walked upon the earth making the most of every encounter. He taught from a boat upon the shores of Galilee, he called to a tax collector up in a tree. He shared his love sitting at a well, at a dinner party, a wedding, in a garden, upon the highways, and byways. He spoke with the sick by the pools of Bethesda, in an upper room, and in the holy temple of God. He preached upon a hillside, and he saved the lost even upon the cross. There was no place where Jesus went that he did not share the truth of himself and the Father. He was always about his Father's business wherever he was, with the sick and the well, the rich and the poor.

Jesus said in John 5:17,23, "My Father is working until now, and I Myself am working," "He who does not honor the Son, does not honor the Father who sent Him." God placed within the heart of every believer a spring of living water so it would flow out and cover all the earth. A spring is not a lone stream for one to drink from but rather it is a life source for the many to take in that they may taste and see that the Lord is good. Jesus spoke this truth to the woman of Samaria in John 4:14, "Whoever drinks of the water that I shall give him shall never thirst: but the water that I shall give him shall become in him a well of water springing up to eternal life." God will order your path to the thirsty, to the weary one who is tired of drinking from the cisterns of the world. He pours into us that we may pour into others.

How many thirsty, wandering in the desert of life, have passed through the corridors of your life whether but for a moment or a lifetime? What well did you draw from to satisfy their thirsty soul? How did you respond to the thirsty one, beloved? Did you pour out into Jesus? What revival we would know and be a part of, if we would take up our water pots daily filled with love and the saving power of Jesus and not come in from the fields until we have poured out every drop. If we had the unstoppable faith and determination that the Apostles had when they were told by the governing authorities not to speak of Jesus anymore saying:

> Whether it is right in the sight of God to give heed to you rather than to God, you be the judge; for we cannot stop peaking what we have seen and heard." And then go on further to pray, "And now Lord, take note of their threats,

and grant that Thy bondservant may speak Thy word with all confidence.

—Acts 4:19–20,29

God answered their prayer. For his word tells us, "And with great power the apostles were giving witness to the resurrection of the Lord Jesus, and abundant grace was upon them all" (John 4:33). If we lack faith, if we lack the boldness that we need to witness to others, then can we not cry out to God just as his apostles did so long ago? Absolutely! We can't even use fear as an excuse because God will give us courage if we would ask. It was not easy to witness during the times of the apostles because the same hatred that crucified Jesus was still alive and well, and the apostles would all fall prey to it according to God's appointed time. Everyone would be martyred for their witness except for John, who was put into a cauldron of hot oil before being exiled on an island called Patmos to live out his remaining years. Witnessing has been costly from the beginning and the price tag hasn't changed over time. Until we determine to not count the cost and step out trusting God to speak through us and depending upon him for the words to speak, we will never know the joy of bringing someone to the Lord.

This is where true joy comes from, a deep abiding joy not in things or accomplishments but through being used by God. As the time of the Lord's return draws near, the pulse of heaven to redeem the lost grows louder, stronger, and more urgent. Listen to the cry of the blessed Prophet Isaiah, "Drip down, O heavens, from above, and let the clouds pour down righteousness; let the earth open up and salvation bear fruit, and righteousness spring up with it…" (Isaiah 45:8). This must become the desire of our heart before we will be overtaken to share the Gospel. All other desires must be swallowed up in this one pursuit, this one driving force if eternity is going to matter to us. It's a vigilant praying for God to stamp eternity before our eyes and cause our hearts to beat as one with his; to break our heart with what breaks his and let not his pressing burden for the lost be lifting from us. The cries of the lost are offered up continuously before the throne of Grace, yet where is the vessel to pour out mercy upon the desperate? We will all spend eternity somewhere, precious one. Every soul that passes through our lives will face the Living God to give an account for their lives. We must make every effort to reach them before that day dawns.

There is such an urgency from the Prophet Isaiah for the salvation of his people. His heart was overturned because of their sin and lack of repentance. He understood fully well that the time to reach them was fleeting, therefore they must be reached at any cost. Where is the burden for the lost condition of our people? How often do we weep for the disgrace of our nation because of its sin? Listen to the heart of the one who did—one who lived this conviction to death. I pray we will gird ourselves continuously with this same conviction for our nation. Hear these words deeply embracing them as the prayer of your life:

> A voice is calling, clear the way for the Lord
> in the wilderness; make smooth in the desert a

highway for our God. Let every valley be lifted up. And every mountain and hill be made low; and let the rough ground become a plain, and the rugged terrain a broad valley; then the glory of the Lord will be revealed, and all flesh will see it together; for the mouth of the Lord has spoken, A voice calls out. Then he answered, "What shall I call out?" All flesh is grass, and its loveliness is like the flower of the field. The grass withers, the flower fades, when the breath of the Lord blows upon it. Surely the people are grass. The grass withers, the flower fades, but the word of our God stands forever. Get yourself upon on a high mountain, O Zion, bearer of good news, life up your voice mightily, O Jerusalem, bearer of good news; Lift it up, do not fear say to the cities of Judah, Here is your God! Behold the Lord God will come with might with His arm ruling for Him. Behold, His reward is with Him, and His recompense before Him.

—Isaiah 40:3–10

Until our prayers are offered in brokenness, overshadowing remorse, and painful intercession for salvation to come, we will never see revival in our land. The cloak of mourning, the ashes of loss across our heart, and the bowing of the head like a reed must be our stance if waves of mercy shall fall upon our people. There are no tears anymore over sin before the altar of God. The repenting soul languishing because of transgression is not found in the house of God. We must mourn, weep, and grieve over sin. We must give him no rest until he rains righteousness upon our land once again. For he gives us this mighty promise, "If my people, who are called by name will humble themselves and pray, seek my face and turn from their wicked ways, then I will hear from Heaven, forgive their sin and will heal their land" (2 Chronicles 7:14).

God wants to extend mercy to us, and he desires to heal our land from the disease of sin. But we must be his witnesses, his voice, and his heart to the people. We must use our voice in witness before man and before God on their behalf. If we pray, then God will increase our burden for the lost and our burden to pray for the lost. Our confidence in witnessing flows out of our confidence in prayer.

The weeping prophet Jeremiah was afraid to speak up and witness for God to his people but God reassures his heart in prayer saying,

> "Do not say that 'I am a youth,' because everywhere I send you, you shall go. And all that I command you, you shall speak. Do not be afraid of them. For I am with you to deliver you, declares the Lord." Then the Lord stretched out His hand and touched my mouth, and the Lord said to me, "Behold, I have put My words in your mouth."
>
> —Jeremiah 1:7-9

Jeremiah was called the weeping prophet because his heart was grieved over the state of his land. His people were in darkness because of their transgressions and disobedience to the God who loved them and had been faithful to them. He mourned with deepness that no ordinary man could have apart from being in the presence of the God who longs to save to the uttermost. The burden for the lost was birthed in his heart in the presence of God. God will do the same for us, if we will stay before him and cry out for our heart to become united with his. But know this, God's heart is heavy for his people, it grieves for the lost and the weight will be more than we can bear. But from our lips will come the fruit of salvation.

God will instill in us a wall against fear, raise up a wall of confidence round about us that comes from him and not from our own abilities because they will fail us in time of need. Speak his words, be obedient to go where he leads, and speak when he commands you and he promises to be with you. Resolve to never fear people, only the Lord in disobedience. He will bless your mouth to speak of his salvation and many will come to a saving knowledge of Jesus Christ through you. There is no better life goal than this, no greater life of joy to be known. Our secret success will come from praying for the lost before we ever speak to the lost. And what do we pray, how do we pray for a country so far away from God? Let us pray the words of Nehemiah for the land God has given us to dwell in:

> I sat down and wept and mourned for days; and I was fasting and praying before the God of heaven. And I said, "I beseech Thee, O Lord God of heaven, the great and awesome God, who preserves the covenant and loving

kindness for those who love Him and keep His commandments."

Let Thine ear now be attentive and Thine eyes open to hear the prayer of Thy servant which I am praying before Thee now, day and night, on behalf of the sons of Israel (America) Thy servants, confessing the sins of the sons of Israel (America) which we have sinned against Thee; I and my father's house have sinned. We have acted very corruptly against Thee and have not kept the commandments nor the statues, nor the ordinances which Thou did command Thy servant Moses.

—Nehemiah 1:4–7

The wonder that God would even use me still sets my soul in awe and thanksgiving. He formed your mouth to speak life, to speak the redeeming name of Jesus. Sharing Jesus with a lost and dying world begins upon our knees and ends on our feet, never the other way around. We must humble ourselves for the lost before God and he will exalt us before them in courage, love, and wisdom from above. He will give us favor beyond measure and he will order every step we take. He will clothe us with honor and gird us about with anointing to proclaim the way of the Lord. For blessed is *she* who comes in the name of the Lord. This is the hour. Rise up and take you place among the saints of old and, without fear, cry out, proclaim, and declare the name that is above every name, *Jesus*.

Please take the time to journal your thoughts. It's rewarding to pen your heart upon paper.

My Prayer and Thoughts:

_____

_____

_____

_____

_____

_____

_____

_____

_____

_____

_____

But the Psalmist said, "And by my God, I shall leap over a wall" (Psalm 18:29).

A Love for His Word

"Oh how I love Thy law! It is my meditation all the day"

—Psalm 119:97

To love God's word is to love him. The two are inseparable. You cannot love one and hate the other, and you cannot love one apart from the other. Soon after I surrendered my life to the lordship of Jesus Christ, by the providence of God, I signed up to take a Bible study at my church. It was a precept study on the book of Philippians led by my precious pastor's wife, Joy. I knew nothing about the book of Philippians, let alone how to study the Bible. I was scared to death when I arrived at the first meeting. All the other ladies were much older than I was and far more mature in the Lord than I ever thought I would be. I barely opened my mouth and that was only to answer when called upon, which I fervently prayed would never happen. I struggled through every week's lesson thinking, *I'm just not getting it.* But at the advice of Sister Joy, I stuck it out until the end. I poured every ounce of my strength into the study genuinely wanting to learn and slowly a light began to shine upon the Scriptures. I hungered to know and understand the Word of God and prayed diligently, "Open my eyes that I may behold wonderful things from Thy Law" (Psalm 119:18). This prayer birthed a love of God's word inside me that would change the course of my life all together. I became an eternal student of the Bible.

The more I learned, the more I discovered I did not know! But this gift of understanding only fueled my passion to know God's Word even more. The following year, I was given the rare privilege of going to stay at Precept Ministries for two weeks and receive further training and reap the benefits of sitting under Kay Arthur in person as we studied the book of Romans together with her. She was writing Romans part 3 when I was there that summer. I saw something in her life that drew me to God himself and even more so to Bible study. Her life was a flame upon which God started a fire in my own that continues to burn to this day. At the time, I did not realize the value, the necessity, and spiritual growth that came from learning God's Word through inductive study. I would come to know its importance later in life when the storms began to rise.

God was using Kay Arthur and I knew why—she was a woman of his Word. She became to me like Paul was to Timothy through her teachings and studies. In looking back, now some thirty years ago, it seems I've only skimmed the surface of God's Word though I've never parted from faithful inductive study. I learned the secret of the Psalmist who said, "How can a young man keep his way pure? By keeping it according to Thy Word. Thy Word I have treasured in my heart, that I may not sin against Thee" (Psalm 119:9,11). The key to walking before God in a way that is pleasing to him is to treasure his word in our heart to keep us from sin. Through his Word, we are kept from sin, protected and guarded. "His Word is a lamp unto our feet and a light unto our path" (Psalm 119:105). It lights the holy path that we should walk and sheds truth upon our feet so we will not stumble in our ways. Without God's Word, we would be hopelessly the slave of sin never able to live in such a way as pleases his heart.

Faithful mining in the Lord's mine of Scripture will produce in us a reverence for him, a fear of sin and a love to serve him. It will grow us beyond anything we could ever imagine and in the process mold us into the very likeness of Jesus who is the Word (John 1:1,14). We cannot become like Jesus if we do not become like the Word. Throughout the span of Scriptures, you will see the greatest promises from God are regarding his Word. It's the only eternal thing we have in this world. He watches over his Word to perform it, to accomplish his purposes as a faithful Watchman upon the walls of glory. His Word reveals who he is, and who he desires us to be, and how to become that woman. Listen carefully, oh daughter, you will never become the woman whom God intends for you to be and never fulfill the plans he has for you apart from the study of his Word. Until you become desperate to know his Word so you can know him, you will cease to grow and will stay in a perpetual holding place in spiritual service for his kingdom.

Upon these pages, I want to inundate you with the truth and power found with the pages of God's Word. We cannot and will not make it, fulfill it, glorify it without his Word in our life.

> Forever, O Lord, Thy word is settled in heaven.
> Thy faithfulness continues throughout all gen-

erations; thou didst establish the earth, and it stands. They stand this day according to Thy Ordinances (His Word)...If Thy law had not been my delight, then I would have perished in my affliction. I will never forget Thy precepts, for by them Thou hast revived me. I am Thine, save me; for I have sought Thy precepts. The wicked wait for me to destroy me; I shall diligently consider Thy testimonies. I have seen a limit to all perfection; Thy commandment is exceedingly broad.

—Psalm 119:89-96

Out of the Psalms comes a truth so mighty, so prevailing that if we would lay hold of it and allow it to lay hold of us, then we would be unshakeable, unstoppable in the war against the kingdom of darkness. The psalmist gives praise to God's Word declaring that if it had not been the delight of his heart in the time of affliction, he would have perished, he wouldn't have made it through. The precepts or truths from the Holy Scriptures are what revived him when he was downtrodden. God's word gives us strength; it builds strong spiritual bones that will hold up under the pressures of life and ministry. Until we learn that we need God's Word in our lives, we will never know how much we need God himself.

Reading our devotions every morning is wonderful and a great spiritual habit to maintain daily but that is not what will feed us in times of spiritual famine. Devotions will help set our mind for the day but a true inductive Bible study, which is done consistently in your life, is the only thing that will mature you in the Lord, building strong roots of faith. The Apostle Paul's words in Romans 10:17 teach us that faith comes by hearing when the hearing is coming from the Word of God. Faith comes from God's Word. It doesn't come by praying for God to give you faith alone, it comes through his Word. God's Word deposits faith into us, building it up over time until we are women who are full of faith in God. God's Word becomes a spiritual oasis for our soul because of fruitful study. When our faith is tested during difficult times, and it will be, and if we do not have a storage house of God's word within us, we will have no resources to protect us from spiritual demise. Experience is not a safe storage house!

We gather in summer because we know that winter will eventually come, and we will need nourishment if we are going to make it through. We must go the way of renunciation before we can go the way of the Living Word. We must have a renounce of all fear of giving up our worldly toys even if they bring about an inward bleeding. We often times will not surrender our things to God because we fear for their safety; we are afraid that he will not do with them what we want him to do. We must part from all that rivals him and hinders us from the journey of knowing him. Our hearts must be determined and committed to settle for nothing less than total abandonment of self to the pursuit of God. The veil of the flesh is the only thing that keeps us outside the Holy of holies, the only thing that blinds us to seeing and knowing God. Expel all that expels his word from your life.

Time and time again when I have sailed through difficult waters, the Words of God hidden down in the deepest recess of my soul will emerge to steady me; to set my sails even against the winds if it means keeping me on course with the Lord. I have seen fear wash away like a flood as peace came washing in over me with all God's breakers of strength and comfort. His precious Word has been a light for me when the way was so dark that I did not know which way to go. It has cradled me in its strong unfailing arms and hushed my crying, wiping away every tear. His Word has never misled me, never forsook me in my time of need and never once stood silent when I cried out for wisdom but answered valiantly, "Thus sayeth the Lord." When I was battered by the cruelty of others, it has anchored me in with the love and abiding presence of God. As I have held the broken in my arms, it has placed the words of God's grace upon my tongue to soothe the aching heart. When the devil has robbed me of my peace, the Word has reminded me of what I know to be true about my God. It has been my faithful companion for over thirty years and when I have turned my heart to search for truth, it has been there as a bulwark of hope and strength. His Word has been the lover of my soul, the balm of Gilead for every hurt and the peace of God through every trial. It has never wavered, never failed this woman.

I've witnessed the power of God's Word, not only in my own life, but in the lives of countless women over the years. I've seen them transformed right before my eyes by the washing of the water of his Word. The

Word of God changes us, transforms, and reforms us. Listen to the writer of Hebrews, "For the Word of God is living and active and sharper than any two-edged sword, and piercing as far as the division of soul and spirit, of both joints and marrow, and able to judge the thoughts and intentions of the hear" (Hebrews 4:12). Powerful is the word of God, beloved! Jeremiah 23:29 declares, "Is not my word like fire? Declares the Lord, and like a hammer which shatters a rock?" Do you want the fire of God in your life? Do you want God to build you up into the mighty woman of God you know he wants you to become? His Word is the answer—it will never happen apart from his Word. Listen to Peter's words to us:

> For you have been born again not of seed which is perishable but imperishable, that is, through the living and abiding word of God. For, all flesh is like grass, and all its glory like the flower of grass, the grass withers and the flower falls off but the word of the Lord abides forever...Therefore putting aside all malice and all guile and hypocrisy and envy and all slander, like newborn babes, long for the pure milk of the word, that by it you may grow in respect to salvation.
>
> —1 Peter 1:23–2:2

The pure milk of the Word grows us up in Christ. It cultivates our relationship with him, it reveals God to us, and trains us in how to live righteous on the face of the earth. It will never fade and long after you are gone, it will continue its working power.

Every woman or man that God has used mightily upon the earth has been life-long students of God's Word. If we are not filling our hearts with his truth, then what will we have to pour out upon those who are in need of it? It's amazing to see so many struggling to accomplish the work of God through earthly wisdom, fleshly tactics. We ask God to bless us in our teaching, in our ministries, but lack the love and study of his Word in our lives. Much of the work is being done apart from diligent study of God's words deeming it as unnecessary to succeed in ministry. But Paul instructs Timothy that, "All scripture is inspired by God and profitable for teaching, for reproof, for correction, for training in righteousness; that the man (or woman) of God may be adequate, equipped for every good work" (2 Timothy 3:16–17). Our adequacy, our equipping for every good work comes from Scripture. If we want our ministries to prosper, then the Word of God is the answer, not better programs, methodology, or more talented willing members.

I'm in no way minimizing prayer because it is vital to the increase of God's Kingdom and we've seen that in scripture already in previous chapters. But prayer without the word is powerless prayer. The two must be combined. We can pray all we want but until we open up his Word and begin to breathe him in through the study of his pages our praying will linger upon the floor upon which they were given. Listen to the heart of the apostles when the church of God was being birthed, "But we will devote ourselves to prayer and the ministry of the Word" (Acts 6:4).

From the very beginning God has shown that his Word is necessary to bring forth life. We see this in Genesis when God spoke and there was light. His word brings forth light and it brings forth life. Apart from his Word, there will be no light in your life or light in your ministry or life. Get this truth, precious, and you will find your spiritual walk and service take off in blazing glory for God.

As a young student of God's Word and a young Christian, I discovered realities about myself that I would have never seen otherwise. God's word is like the smith's fire turning up the heat upon our earthly being until the dross exposes itself before us. It sifts, refines, extracts, and polishes us, breaking up every ounce of barren land. This is often why we don't stick with Bible study when we start it. It may be exciting at first as we begin to learn new things but before long you find that something within you yearns to align itself with the truth of what you are learning. This longing grows stronger until either you yield to its desire or you break away from it altogether trying to silence its voice. The Spirit of God within you, as a born-again Christian, will always yield to the Word of God because they are one with each other. They are in perfect harmony because they can do nothing less. When we struggle against this reality, we lose inner peace and often choose to escape from the war.

There is such honor and provision poured out and promised to the righteous one. King David loved the Word of God as seen in his writings:

153

The righteous will inherit the land, and dwell in it forever. The mouth of the righteous utters wisdom, and his tongue speaks justice. The law of God is in his heart; His steps do not slip.

—Psalm 37:29–30

And once again he declares, "The law of the Lord is perfect, restoring the soul; the testimony of the Lord is sure, making wise the simple. The precepts of the Lord are right, rejoicing the heart; the commandment of the Lord is pure, enlightening the eyes. The fear of the Lord is clean, enduring forever; the judgments of the Lord are true; they are righteous altogether. They are more desirable than gold, yes, than much fine gold; sweeter also than honey and the drippings of the honeycomb. Moreover by them Thy servant is warned; in keeping them there is great reward."

—Psalm 19:7–11

David knew the secret to the spiritual giants of the earth—a love for the law of God. He feared the loss of it, so that he would rather die than to lose its print before him. He clung to the precepts of God as if clinging to life itself. He knew it was his guard, his light and protector from all the enemies who surrounded him continuously. He knew that he could not please God apart from his Word and more importantly by God's Word, David received God's favor. Even at the end of David's life, even though he had sinned against God, he was still given the title as God's anointed—the apple of his eye. And how did he become the apple of

God's eye? It is because he loved his Word. There was nothing he loved more than the holy pages of God's heart revealed to man. So great was his love for the Word that God allowed David's love songs to become part of its pages.

The more you read and study the word of God, the more you will long for it, yearn for more of it. It will become to you like breathing; something you cannot live without once it has given you life. There is no substitute for diligent Bible study, none. You will of course benefit from the teaching and preaching of others, but the greatest spiritual harvest in your life will come from the fields of Holy Scripture. You will find God there, always, waiting and longing to meet with you, and fellowship with you, teaching you his ways that you may know him. You will receive the fullness of God's heart upon its sacred pages—his breath has been upon every word. They are life to your bones, strength to your age, comfort for your pain, guidance for today, and your hope for tomorrow. It will clothe you in confidence yet gird you about with the sweetness of humility. You will be strong and courageous, full of faith, and showing no fear before man. You will have no dread of the future or present circumstances because the word is the blanket of sovereignty draped across your soul.

His Word beckons you, waits for you, and calls to you even this hour. What reprieve will you give to its demand? Will you rise to the challenge given by Paul to Timothy that says, "Study to show thyself approved unto God, a workman needing not to be ashamed" (2 Timothy 2:15)? Will you gird yourself about with the belt of truth so you will be able to stand firm against the enemy. What answer, what place will you give to the Bible? Many claim it's the truth; many claim it's the Word of God himself, but few give themselves to its study. Our greatest limits to becoming the woman God will use is giving ourselves to prayer and to the study of Scripture. As long as we are satisfied with giving little to God, he will be satisfied to give little to us. The more we give to him, the more he will give to us. The more we study the Word, the more truth he will pour into us; and the more he pours into us, the more he can pour out through us.

People ask me all the time, "How do you do it? How do you work full time and yet still have time to study God's word like you do?" My answer is simple: I make time for the things that are important to me, and I have no choice but to give my time to those things that I can't live without. I can't live without water, without food and rest. So it is with studying God's Word for me, I can't live without it. It's not just a love for me, it's a necessity. My life is utterly dependent upon it, and apart from it, I would surely die spiritually. I'm no good to anyone if I'm out of his Word. It's the same with all of us; we are no good to anyone without the Word of God increasing in our lives. If you are not a student, a dedicated student of study to the Word of God, he will not use you as he could, as he wants to. You will always limit his power and working in and through you as long as you ignore the study of God's Word. Many people want the crown of God's approval in service but few make the needed sacrifice of Bible study that grace the brow of God's child.

As long as you are content with simple, quick devotions in the morning that last all from five to ten minutes usually skimming the surface of God's Word, then you will only skim the surface of God's best for you. When someone is not being used by God, it's usually a result of one of three things or all three—sin, prayerlessness, and no study of the Word. Don't settle for meritocracy in living. Stretch and run the race set before you, applying all diligence to prayer and the relentless, passionate study of God's Holy Word. If you love him, you will love his Word. If you love his Word, then you will love him. The sweeter journey lies within the ancient pages of Scripture. Your heart will sing over them as you savor every truth, every word breathed from the very mouth of God. Every word has a heartbeat and it will overpower your own until only one beat is heard.

I want to close out our chapter together with some encouraging words of hope for all of you who may think you don't have what it takes to study the Bible or that you are too young in the Lord to take that on. Don't listen to any of those negative thoughts—cast them out of your mind. Know that God has placed his spirit within you, and he is the one who gives your mind understanding, not you. You don't have to rely on your own intellect. If we did, then I would be in grave danger! I would have been a lost cause before the Lord even started with me. It's not about brain size but heart size! He will instruct you, He will teach you and speak to you wonderful truths hidden to the ordinary eye. You will confound even the wise with your wisdom because you have learned from the One Who is wisdom. You will shine like the greatest star on the darkest night and all for his glory.

A woman once came in my office and during the course of our conversation about the Lord, she spoke these all inspiring words, "If I never say another word, I want my life to be a living Scripture." That's what Scripture should be—precious, living, and active. The world longs to see living Scripture. If you would but dare to be that woman, you will captivate the world by the mystery of your spiritual beauty because they will wonder from where it came. Your feet will walk securely and will not slip even though all may fall around you. In you, the light of Jesus will radiate the glow of promise, the glory of God, and the beauty of his salvation because the Word is living, abiding with you. There will be no thievery of peace because the Words of the one who is peace sustains your inward being. Your lamp will never go out, and the sun rising upon your face will set warmly and confidently upon your brow. Though a host encamps round about you, you will have no fear because his word will hedge you in with the truth of his protecting power. You will never lack counsel, for the wonderful Counselor has made your heart his dwelling place. The life you live will give hope to many. It will rescue, save, deliver, and exhort all who long to know that God is there. Become the living Scripture the world longs to see. May it burn within you as an all consuming sweet and holy madness until only the living Word is seen and heard from your beating heart.

My Thoughts and Prayer:

A Passion for the Anointing

> Now the God of hope fill you with all joy and
> peace in believing, that ye may abound in hope,
> through the power of the Holy Ghost.
>
> —Romans 15:13

A multitude of books have been written about the anointing of God and countless opinions spoken regarding it down through the ages. It's a subject that few dare to make claim as having a complete handle of—myself at the top of that list. So I make no claim to be an authority, actually far from it, but I do claim to be a seeker of it—one who yearns for it continually. I struggle even now praying for every word to write here upon these pages, for I believe we are venturing upon a most holy subject—the anointing of God. Words cannot capture a description worthy of it but when someone has it, it's clear for all to see. The best definition is one that is seen in living form. The anointing is not an emotion, although it is felt to the deepest part of each of us. It's altogether strange and wonderfully supernatural. We never know when we might encounter its presence, but when it happens, our souls are at home. Once you have experienced it, you are ruined forever—nothing else will satisfy.

To do the work of the Lord, one must have the Lord doing the work, or all is in vain. The world is desperate— the church is desperate for the anointing of God to manifest itself through his servants. Our spiritual lands are ever barren for lack of the later rains, the anointing poured out without measure upon the ruins of the earth. Unless the presence of God falls, there will be no revival, no harvest of souls, no deliverance, no peace, no victory, and the kingdom of darkness will continue its reign dragging with it souls into an eternal hell. We cannot continue to teach, preach, serve, witness, pray, or do any other work for God in the flesh as if that is good enough. It will never suffice for the need of the hour which is far greater than our resources.

There must be awakening to the need of God's anointing, a recognition that something is missing in our midst. We must rise from our slumbering state of complacency and mediocrity, believing that there is more. Our eyes must turn away from our traditions, denominations, condemnations, and frustrations, and look to the hills of God from whence cometh our help. It's our duty to renounce all of the flesh, including our spiritual service to God in the church and world. Until this complete renunciation takes place in us, the anointing cannot and will not come upon our lives. If you long to be used by God, this is the lifeline of all that God can and will do in and through you. Your measure of usefulness will be determined by the measure of God's power resting upon you.

There are many who believe that the anointing of the Holy Spirit or the baptism of the Holy Spirit and the indwelling of the Spirit are both one in the same. I was taught to believe that when one comes to Christ, they receive all of the Holy Spirit they are going to get.

I have struggled with this for years because as a student of God's Word, I saw there was a difference in having the indwelling of the Holy Spirit and a baptism of the Holy Spirit or as we will refer to it as God's anointing. I became a seeker of truth and discovered that all the while, I was a seeker of the power from on high that I was increasingly aware that I did not possess. My heart refused to settle for fleshy works which will be burned up in the later days amounting to a wasted life. Was there more to salvation than forgiveness of sins and security of eternal life with God? Did God want more from me? Did he want to do more through me and in me? I ask that you bear with me in this journey of truth even if you don't agree, beloved. I ask that you remove the glasses of your traditions, denominational beliefs, and opinions formed long ago by the influences you have been exposed to. Journey with me a little further before closing the book.

I love to soak in the writings of spiritual giants such as D.L. Moody, Spurgeon, Wesley, Finney, Torrey, Tozer, Lettie Cowman, Mueller, and others who have burned a path with their faith for us to follow. I have found in my devouring of literature over the years concerning these great men and women of God that God is just as ready to use me and you and anyone who would dare yield themselves to the divine power of the Holy Spirit. There are plenty in Christendom to do the talking and criticizing but few who are willing, longing to be clothed with the power from on high. I remember reading a story once about Mr. Moody's encounter with

God's anointing. It is this event that changed the course of my service, ministry to and for God.

D.L. Moody was approached by two elderly ladies that had been attending his services every night during a tent revival. Each night they spoke the same words to Mr. Moody, "We're praying for you." This statement began to agitate Mr. Moody, wondering why they weren't interceding for the lost to be saved instead, so one night he asked them, "Why are you praying for me?" They replied, "We are praying that you will receive the power." He thought on this for a while and when he could stand it no longer, he went to their home that he might speak with them further and to pray together. That night they prayed, including Moody for the baptism of the Holy Spirit to fall upon him. The sisters testified that they had never heard such groaning in prayer as Moody prayed that night pleading for God's power to fall upon him. It was as earnest a prayer as heaven had ever heard, no doubt.

Not long after that night Moody was walking down Wall Street in New York City when the Spirit of God began to fall upon him. It was so strong that Moody had to run to a nearby friend's house asking to have a room where he might pray and get alone with God. He stayed in there for hours as the anointing from on high fell. It kept falling and pouring upon him. He was full of inexpressible joy, and finally when he could not take anymore, he had to ask God to relent because if he did not, Moody thought he would surely die from the force of joy that was flooding his body. He left for revival meetings in London the next day and the power of God was so heavy upon him that hundreds upon hundreds were saved. His life and ministry were never the same.

Some say that when the baptism of the Holy Spirit or the anointing falls upon a person, they will speak in tongues as a sign that the Spirit of God has indeed fallen. According to Scripture, this is not always the case. The Apostle Paul is a living example of this. He fell upon his face on the road to Damascus, seeing Jesus himself and was miraculously saved and gloriously called and commissioned into service for God. Paul did not speak in tongues nor are we told he did afterwards. Paul did not receive this gift of tongues, but he did lose the gift of sight for a few days. We are told he fasted and prayed for three days during this ordeal. But glimpse with me the power of his ministry described in his own words. Read them very carefully, beloved, so you won't miss vital truth to our topic.

> And when I came to you, brethren, I did not come with superiority of speech or of wisdom, proclaiming to you the testimony of God, for I determined to know nothing among you except Jesus Christ, and Him crucified. I was with you in weakness and in fear and in much trembling, and my message and my preaching were not in persuasive words of wisdom, but in demonstration of the Spirit and of power, so that your faith would not rest on the wisdom of men, but on the power of God.
>
> —1 Corinthians 2:1–5

Paul speaks of his conversion and the working of God through him as two separate and yet necessary events.

He also says, "But we have this treasure in earthen vessels, that the excellency of the power may be of God, and not of us" (2 Corinthians 4:7, KJV). Paul makes it clear that there are two different kinds of power—fleshly and godly. The excellent power is the power that is from God. It's this excellency of the power of God that Elisha longed for and travailed until the very end to obtain. It's the same power that fell on the day of Pentecost to the believers who were waiting. It's the same anointing that John the Baptist had crying, "Behold the Lamb of God Who takes away the sins of the world"(John 1:29). It's the same anointing Stephen, the first martyr of the Church had as his face glowed with the presence of God even as he was dying. It's the power that parted the Red Sea, brought water from a rock, manna in the desert, fire from heaven, and rain on command. Salvation and the anointing are separate events in a believer's life. But it is this anointing that every believer must have if they are to live fruitful lives for God.

The Apostle Paul knew this difference. Listen to his heart once again as he writes to the body of believers in the city of Corinth, "And he said unto me, My grace is sufficient for thee: for my strength is made perfect in weakness. Most gladly therefore will I glory in my infirmities, that the power of Christ may rest upon me" (2 Corinthians 12:9, KJV). It's that one little word "that" in this sentence we cannot deny. It implies a choice or an alternative way. The apostle knows that there is a power that comes from Christ that can rest upon us and there is a natural power of the flesh. He is not speaking of the Holy Spirit living in him because

Paul is already a born again Christian when he wrote this letter. His conversion, the indwelling of the Holy Spirit, and the power of Christ resting upon him are something altogether different even though they are one in the same in source. He sees the trials of sickness as a means by which God's power can be increased in his life; they can cause the power of God to rest upon him. Have you ever wondered why Paul's life was used by God in such magnitude or thought about how many books are in the New Testament and the majority of them were written by Paul? The answer to his amazing ministry was God's anointing resting upon him.

Listen to other writings of Paul where this same truth pours forth; he wants God's children to understand the difference so they too will long for God's anointing upon their lives. To the Church of Philippi he writes, "That I may know him, and the power of his resurrection, and the fellowship of his sufferings, being made conformable unto his death," (Philippians 3:10, KJV). After walking with the Lord for over forty years, his cry is to know the power of Jesus's resurrection in the fullest. He had the power of God upon his life, yet he never ceased from wanting it all the more. He was desperate for it, pleaded for it, and would not settle for anything less than the full anointing of God resting on him. I would ask you, precious daughter, have you settled? Maybe you've known the touch of God before or in times past but have failed to continue to plead with the heavens to continue the flow of it. It's time to begin pleading, time is short, is very short.

Paul tells the church in Thessalonica, "For our gospel came not unto you in word only, but also in power, and in the Holy Ghost, and in much assurance; as ye know what manner of men we were among you for your sake" (Thessalonians 1:5, KJV). Oh, that gospel would not come in word only today, but also in power and in the Holy Ghost. The gospel can come in word only, as we see in Paul's words, but he had chosen the higher road, the road less traveled in ministry, the road of power and of the Holy Ghost. And a second time he says to them, "Wherefore also we pray always for you, that our God would count you worthy of this calling, and fulfill all the good pleasure of his goodness, and the work of faith with power" (2 Thessalonians 1:11, KJV). Paul's prayer was for them to have the work of faith with power. He was not praying for a work of faith in itself but rather a work of faith with power or with the anointing. Heaven doesn't come to earth cheap, it never has. The price is always great and far more costly than we ever expected to pay.

The anointing of God is not for sale, for no price can be placed upon God himself. His anointing cannot be obtained through manipulation, through persuasion, a program or method, and not even through giftedness— it's God's gift to give and his to remove. But it is our gift to seek, to long, and even pursue. Nothing great is obtained with ease but with striving and constant relentless pursuit. A woman who has made the anointing her life's passion will become God's passion to the world. I want to be very intentional in persuading you with all the confidence of heaven to take this less-traveled road; choose it and your life will be all the better for it. D.L. Moody had a passion, after tasting

the anointing of God, for all of God's children to have
the same anointing. The anointing is not meant for just
us, beloved, but all of God's children. Let me share a
story of one such event in Moody's life as told by R.A.
Torrey in a sermon he once preached. I have selected
this out of the archives of his sermons and there are no
constraints on publishing its contents so I share them
giving full credit to the preaching of R.A. Torrey:

> I shall never forget the eighth of July 1894,
> to my dying day. It was the closing day of
> the Northfield Students' Conference—the
> gathering of the students from the eastern
> colleges. Mr. Moody had asked me to preach
> on Saturday night and Sunday morning on the
> baptism with the Holy Ghost. On Saturday
> night I had spoken about, "The Baptism With
> the Holy Ghost: What It Is; What It Does;
> the Need of It and the Possibility of It." On
> Sunday morning I spoke on "The Baptism
> With the Holy Spirit: How to Get It." It was
> just exactly twelve o'clock when I finished my
> morning sermon, and I took out my watch and
> said, "Mr. Moody has invited us all to go up to
> the mountain at three o'clock this afternoon to
> pray for the power of the Holy Spirit. It is three
> hours to three o'clock. Some of you cannot wait
> three hours. You do not need to wait. Go to
> your rooms; go out into the woods; go to your
> tent; go anywhere where you can get alone with
> God and have this matter out with Him.
>
> At three o'clock, we all gathered in front
> of Mr. Moody's mother's house (she was then

still living), and then began to pass down the lane, through the gate, up on the mountainside. There were four hundred and fifty-six of us in all; I know the number because Paul Moody counted us as we passed through the gate.

After a while Mr. Moody said, "I don't think we need to go any further; let us sit down here." We sat down on stumps and logs and on the ground. Mr. Moody said, "Have any of you students anything to say?" I think about seventy-five of them arose, one after the other, and said, "Mr. Moody, I could not wait till three o'clock; I have been alone with God since the morning service, and I believe I have a right to say that I have been baptized with the Holy Spirit."

When these testimonies were over, Mr. Moody said, "Young men, I can't see any reason why we shouldn't kneel down here right now and ask God that the Holy Ghost may fall upon us just as definitely as He fell upon the apostles on the Day of Pentecost. Let us pray." And we did pray, there on the mountainside. As we had gone up the mountainside heavy clouds had been gathering, and just as we began to pray, those clouds broke and the raindrops began to fall through the overhanging pines. But there was another cloud that had been gathering over Northfield for ten days, a cloud big with the mercy and grace and power of God; and as we began to pray, our prayers seemed to pierce that cloud and the Holy Ghost fell upon us. Men and women that is what we all need: the Baptism with the Holy Ghost."

D.L. Moody was right, beloved one, we all need it. We all need the fire of God so desperately, for without it, righteousness will never fall from the skies above washing over our sin-stained land to cleanse it and purge it for the glory of God. If there is a lack of this fire upon the earth, it is not the world we should place the blame, it is the church, you, and me. The fire only falls upon sacrifice. The bride of Christ has adorned herself with comfort, notoriety, the praise of others, and the accomplishments of ministry. She is easily divided over meaningless things, warring over the minute rather than souls who are on their way to an eternal hell. She would rather sell the world on her programs, methods, and on church membership than sell them on Jesus. Because there is no sacrifice upon the altar of our lives, there is no fire. The fire is everything—we must be desperate for the fire to fall. We must fight for it, die for it, and settle for nothing less. We have retired from the battle never having been upon the fighting lines. We are too busy to pray, too busy to serve, and too prideful to need the power of God in our lives. We would rather have a method, a program, or title than seek the power, rely upon it, and fight for it. There is no glory for the flesh when God's power is working through us. Here in lies the problem for many. Until we are resolved to the fact that it is God who gets all the glory, we will never look to him to do the work through us. How will he get the glory if the flesh is doing the work?

The meaning of anointing has been described as flesh doing what flesh cannot do in and of itself apart from God. There is no explanation other than God when his anointing is taking place. It is God clothed in human flesh revealing himself to the world. Even Jesus had God's anointing upon his flesh, listen to the words of Isaiah 61:1, words Jesus read in the temple when he walked the earth as a man:

> The Spirit of the Lord God is upon me because the LORD has anointed me to bring good news to the poor. He has sent me to bind up the brokenhearted, to proclaim liberty to the captives, and the opening of the prison to those who are bound to proclaim the year of the LORD's favor, and the day of vengeance of our God; to comfort all who mourn to grant to those who mourn in Zion—to give them a beautiful headdress instead of ashes, the oil of gladness instead of mourning, the garment of praise instead of a faint spirit; that they may be called oaks of righteousness, the planting of the LORD, that he may be glorified. They shall build up the ancient ruins; they shall raise up the former devastations; they shall repair the ruined cities, the devastations of many generations.

The word for Messiah and Christ both mean "Anointed One or Anointed." Anointed itself in both Hebrew and Greek means to smear, to touch, to stroke with one's hand or to cover with one's hand. The meaning shows us that anointing is completely different in meaning than indwelling as when a person becomes a Christian. In 2 Kings 2:9, Elisha asked Elijah for a double portion of his spirit to rest upon him, yet Elisha had already been chosen and pulled out for God's service. Elisha had learned from his mentor that more than calling was necessary; he needed the anointing of Elijah upon his life and a double portion of it. And he was bound not to give up until he had received it. We need this stance of mentality if we are going to receive more from God, do more for God and have God do more through us. Your calling of God upon your life was not ordinary so why should your service to him be? We cannot expect our life to have any impact upon the generation we live in if we are not first impacting with the Spirit of the Living God.

Elisha did twice the miracles Elijah did, and even after he died, his bones still possessed the power of God, enough to bring a dead body back to life because it was laid in the same burial cave. Your anointing from God can even continue on after you have died because God's work is eternal, and it continues long after we are gone and long after the works of the flesh have ceased. Read the account of King David's anointing and how his life changed because of it:

> Invite Jesse to the sacrifice, and I will show you what to do. You are to anoint for me the one I indicate.
> So Samuel took the horn of oil and anointed him in the presence of his brothers, and from that day on the Spirit of the Lord came upon David in power. Samuel then went to Ramah.
>
> —2 Samuel 16:3,13 (NIV)

God on flesh doing the work that flesh cannot do is a powerful description of what it means to have

God's anointing. David was a living example of this truth and did things he would not have been able to do as an ordinary man. Our life can also be such as David's was if you are willing to pay the price. If you wish to live ordinary, giving only the bare minimum to God so you can live the life of your dreams here upon this earth then the anointing is not for you. It will not seek you out and neither will you seek for it. Until you have become miserable in this life, you will never long for eternity. You must hate the things of the world to love the things of God. He must hold your heart, capture your affections, and wrap all that you are up in all that he is. This is the beginning of the new journey of service, of being used by God. You will never be disappointed. I've never read or heard anyone who lived a life of having God's anointing say, "I wish I had not chosen that life." Even those who suffered because of their service to him never once regretted their choices. God never disappoints, never.

We need his precious all-fulfilling power unleashed with us. Look at 2 Corinthians 4:7 with me using the New Living Translation, "However, we possess this precious treasure, the divine Light of the Gospel in frail, human vessels of earth, that the grandeur and exceeding greatness of the power may be shown to be from God and not from ourselves." God gives to his servants his anointing as proof that the works they do are from him and not from themselves. This sacred anointing is given to guard the glory of God, which he shares with no one except the Son. It restrains the flesh from prideful undertakings and boasting of its own accomplishments. The anointing was given in grace to us by God for serving and worshiping him. It's available to every frail human vessel of the earth that has within it the abiding presence of the Holy Spirit. The moment we surrender ourselves unto the Spirit's control, the anointing is poured out not for the glory of the vessel but for the maker of the vessel. This is what makes the anointing beautiful, sacred, and rare, and yes, it will even endow the lowly vessel with the outward grace of God's presence. It will not pour itself out through a prideful vessel, a vessel that seeks its own way or to carry out its own plans. Read with me the words of John the beloved of Jesus:

> But you have been anointed by [you hold a sacred appointment from, you have been given an unction from] the Holy One, and you all know [the Truth] or you know all things. But as for you, the anointing (the sacred appointment, the unction) which you received from Him abides [permanently] in you; [so] then you have no need that anyone should instruct you. But just as His anointing teaches you concerning everything and is true and is no falsehood, so you must abide in (live in, never depart from) Him [being rooted in Him, knit to Him], just as [His anointing] has taught you [to do]. And now, little children, abide (live, remain permanently) in Him, so that when He is made visible, we may have and enjoy perfect confidence (boldness, assurance) and not be ashamed and shrink from Him at His coming.

> —1 John 2:20, 27 (NLT)

Those who will not shrink back when the Lord comes upon the clouds of glory will be the ones whose image is hidden in Christ. Face to face, the face of Christ beholding the face of Christ, is the greatest honor we can give him. Jesus told his disciples, "If you've seen me, you've seen the Father" (John 14:9). Jesus longs for the Father to be seen, to bring him honor, to magnify him in all things. This is why he longs to see himself in you and in me. When he comes, may he see, as if beholding in a mirror, himself in you, precious one, radiantly confident. His precious anointing is the most vital need we have as Christians. We don't need more talent, more gifts, bigger positions, more funding, more people—we need more anointing. All we need is him, indwelling and working through us in the fullest measure. It's all about him, it's all for him, it's all because of him, and it's all by him. This is God's heart, his plan and his way.

> What if every woman everywhere pursued holiness, surrendered to Calvary, and took up the cross of Jesus?

> What if every woman everywhere prayed relentlessly, gave unceasingly, and loved unconditionally?

> What if every woman everywhere longed for heaven, yearned for God, and grieved for the lost?

> What if every woman everywhere fell at the feet of Jesus, poured out herself in wreckless

abandon, and declared her unfailing love for him?

What if every woman everywhere refused to settle, witnessed without shame, and stood for righteousness?

What if every woman everywhere gave heaven no rest—crucified self that Christ might live— put both hands upon the holy plow, planted both feet upon the Rock of ages, fixed her gaze upon the Author and Perfector of her faith, took up the mantle of Elijah, and never looked back?

What if that woman was you?

There is much to do and time is fleeting valiantly in the firmaments. For such a time as this, we have been given the breath of life, a voice to lift and hands to serve. Listen to Jesus's promise to his disciples, "Truly I say to you, whatever you bind on earth shall have been bound in heaven; and whatever you loose on earth shall have been loosed in heaven" (Matthew 18:18). Loose Jesus in your life, and all of heaven will loose him upon the earth in you in power and might, and the world will sing the Father's praises. Give him all of you, hold nothing back from him and surrender all that keeps you from becoming the woman you know he desires for you to be. He longs to use you as an instrument of his grace and mercy. He has a plan, a wonderful magnificent plan for your life. It will mean trusting him in all things, when the way is hard and no light can be found. It will mean absolute consecration giving him even the most sacred and dearest things your heart may have. The way is narrow, steep, and costly, but it leads to His glory. Choose this road, precious daughter, and you will have no regrets when the sun is sinking upon your most beautiful life.

The Story Yet Untold

There is a story yet untold and the author Lord is You,
What will you make of my life and with it what will
   you do?

In the deepest part of my heart, You've penned love's
   sweetest song,
It's the story of our journey to be sung through
   eternity long.

I know not where this journey will take me or what
   the future will hold
Abandoned at Thy feet I lay, for the story yet untold.

Be Thou my vision sweet Lord 'til eternity slips into
   view,
Herald our song at the Portals of Glory for it will
   lead me home to You

When my story is told I will have no regrets for
   what I have done

It will be Heaven's crown of glory, my love song for
Thy Son

❦

—Pam Jenkins

Now to Him who is able to do far more abundantly
beyond all that we ask or think, according to the
power that works within us, to Him be the glory
in the church and in Christ Jesus to all generations
forever and ever. Amen.

—Ephesians 3:20–21

Much love for you,
Pam

My Thoughts to Him:

_____

_____

_____

_____

_____

_____

_____

_____

_____

_____